Gustav Vasa

Paul Watson

Published 2017 by Jovian Press

10 9 8 7 6 5 4 3 2 1 0 00 000 0

CONTENTS

CHILDHOOD AND YOUTH OF GUSTAV VASA. 1496-1513.

THE manor of Lindholm lies in the centre of a smiling district about twenty miles north of the capital of Sweden. Placed on a height between two fairy lakes, it commands a wide and varied prospect over the surrounding country. The summit of this height was crowned, at the close of the fifteenth century, by a celebrated mansion. Time and the ravages of man have long since thrown this mansion to the ground; but its foundation, overgrown with moss and fast crumbling to decay, still marks the site of the ancient structure, and from the midst of the ruins rises a rough-hewn stone bearing the name Gustav Vasa. On this spot he was born, May 12, 1496. The estate was then the property of his grandmother, Sigrid Baner, with whom his mother was temporarily residing, and there is no reason to think it continued long the home of the young Gustav.

The family from which Gustav sprang had been, during nearly a hundred years, one of the foremost families of Sweden. Its coat-of-arms consisted of a simple *vase*, or bundle of sticks; and the Vasa estate, at one time the residence of his ancestors, lay only about ten miles to the north of Lindholm. The first Vasa of whom anything is definitely known is Kristiern Nilsson, the great-grandfather of Gustav. This man became noted in the early part of the fifteenth century as an ardent monarchist, and under Erik held the post of chancellor. After the fall of his master, in 1436, his office was taken from him, but he continued to battle for the cause of royalty until his death. Of the chancellor's three sons, the two eldest followed zealously in the footsteps of their father. The other, Johan Kristersson, though in early life a stanch supporter of King Christiern, and one of the members of his Cabinet, later married a sister of Sten Sture, and eventually embraced the Swedish cause. Birgitta, the wife of Johan Kristersson, is said to have been descended from the ancient Swedish kings. The youngest son of Johan and Birgitta was Erik Johansson, the father of Gustav. Of Erik's early history we know little more than that he married Cecilia, daughter of Magnus Karlsson and Sigrid Baner, and settled at Rydboholm, an estate which he inherited from his father. To this place, beautifully situated on an arm of the Baltic, about ten miles northeast of the capital, Cecilia returned with her little boy from Lindholm; and here Gustav spent the first years of his childhood.

Sweden at this period was in a state of anarchy. In order to appreciate the exact condition of affairs, it will be necessary to cast a glance at some political developments that had gone before. Sweden was originally a confederation of provinces united solely for purposes of defence. Each province was divided into several counties, which were constituted in the main alike. Every inhabitant—if we except the class of slaves, which was soon abolished—was either a landowner or a tenant. The tenants were freemen who owned no land of their own, and hence rented the land of others. All landowners possessed the same rights, though among them were certain men of high birth, who through their large inheritances were much more influential than the rest. Matters concerning the inhabitants of one county only were regulated by the county assemblies, to which all landowners in the county, and none others, were admitted. These assemblies were called and presided over by the county magistrate, elected by general vote at some previous assembly. All law cases arising in the county were tried before the assembly, judgment being passed, with consent of the assembly, by the county magistrate, who was expected to know and expound the traditional law of his county. Questions concerning the inhabitants of more than one county were regulated by the provincial assemblies, composed of all landowners in the province, and presided over by the provincial magistrate, elected by all the landowners in his province. The power of the provincial magistrate in the province was similar to that of the county magistrate in the county; and to his judgment, with consent of the assembly, lay an appeal from every decision of the county magistrates. Above all the provinces was a king, elected originally by the provincial assembly of Upland, though in order to gain the allegiance of the other provinces he was bound to appear before their individual assemblies and be confirmed by them. His duty was expressed in the old formula, "landom råda, rike styre, lag styrke, och frid hålla," which meant nothing more than that he was to protect the provinces from one another and from foreign powers. In order to defray the expense of strengthening the kingdom, he was entitled to certain definite taxes from every landowner, and half as much from every tenant, in the land. These taxes he collected through his courtiers, who in the early days were men of a very inferior class,—mere servants of the king. They lived on the crown estates, which we find in the very earliest times scattered through the land. Besides his right to collect taxes, the king, as general peacemaker, was chief-justice of the realm, and to him lay an appeal from every decision rendered by a provincial magistrate. Such, in brief, was the constitution of Sweden when first known in history.

Christianity, first preached in Sweden about the year 830, brought with it a diminution of the people's rights. When the episcopal dioceses were first marked out, thepeople naturally kept in their own hands the right to choose their spiritual rulers, who were designated *lydbiskopar*, or the people's bishops. But in 1164 the Court of Rome succeeded in establishing, under its own authority, an archbishopric at Upsala; and by a papal bull of 1250 the choice of Swedish bishops was taken from the people and confided to the cathedral chapters under the supervision of the pope. As soon as the whole country became converted, the piety of the people induced them to submit to gross impositions at the hands of those whom they were taught to regard as God's representatives on earth. In 1152 the so-called "Peter's Penning" was established, an annual tax of one penning from every individual to the pope. Besides this, it became the law, soon after, that all persons must pay a tenth of their annual income to the Church, and in addition there were special taxes to the various bishops, deans, and pastors. A still more productive source of revenue to the Church was death-bed piety, through which means a vast amount of land passed from kings or wealthy individuals to the Church. By a law of the year 1200 the clergy were declared no longer subject to be tried for crime in temporal courts; and by the end of the thirteenth century the Church had practically ceased to be liable for crown taxation. It requires but a moment's thought to perceive how heavy a burden all these changes threw on the body of the nation.

Simultaneously with the spread of Christianity still another power began to trample on the liberties of the people. This was the power of the sword. In early times, before civilization had advanced enough to give everybody continuous employment, most people spent their leisure moments in making war. Hence the Swedish kings, whose duty it was to keep the peace, could accomplish that result only by having a large retinue of armed warriors at their command. The expense which this entailed was great. Meantime the crown estates had continually increased in number through merger of private estates of different kings, through crown succession to estates of foreigners dying without descendants in the realm, and through other sources. Some of the kings, therefore, devised the scheme of enlisting the influential aristocracy in their service by granting them fiefs in the crown estates, with right to all the crown incomes from the fief. This plan was eagerly caught at by the aristocrats, and before long nearly all the influential people in the realm were in the service of the king. Thus the position of royal courtier, which had formerly been a mark of servitude, was now counted an honor, the courtiers being now commonly known as magnates. About the year 1200 castles were first erected on some of the crown estates, and the magnates who held these castles as fiefs were not slow to take advantage of their power. Being already the most influential men in their provinces, and generally the county or provincial magistrates, they gradually usurped the right to govern the surrounding territory, not as magistrates of the people, but as grantees of the crown estates. Since these fiefs were not hereditary, the rights usurped by the holders of them passed, on the death of the grantees, to the crown, and in 1276 we find a king granting not only one of his royal castles, but also right of administration over the surrounding land. Thus, by continual enlargement of the royal fiefs, the authority of the provincial assemblies, and even of the county assemblies, was practically destroyed. Still, these assemblies continued to exist, and in them the poor landowners claimed the same rights as the more influential magnates. The magnates, as such, possessed no privileges, and were only powerful because of their wealth, which enabled them to become courtiers or warriors of the king. In 1280, however, a law was passed exempting all mounted courtiers from crown taxation. This law was the foundation of the nobility of Sweden. It divided the old landowners, formerly all equal, into two distinct classes,—the knights, who were the mounted warriors of the king; and the poorer landowners, on whom, together with the class of tenants, was cast the whole burden of taxation. With the progress of time, exemption from crown taxation was extended to the sons of knights unless, on reaching manhood, they failed to serve the king with horse. The knights were thus a privileged and hereditary class. Those of the old magnates who did not become knights were known as armigers, or armor-clad foot-soldiers. The armigers also became an hereditary class, and before long they too were exempted from crown taxation. In many cases the armigers were raised to the rank of knights. Thus the wealthy landowners increased in power, while the poor, who constituted the great body of the nation, grew ever poorer. Many, to escape the taxes shifted to their shoulders from the shoulders of the magnates, sank into the class of tenants, with whom, indeed, they now had much in common. The sword had raised the strong into a privileged aristocracy, and degraded the weak into a down-trodden peasantry.

The aristocracy and the Church,—these were the thorns that sprang up to check the nation's growth. Each had had the same source,—a power granted by the people. But no sooner were they independent of their benefactors, than they made common cause in oppressing the peasantry who had given them birth. They found their point of union in the Cabinet. This was originally a body of men whom the king summoned whenever he needed counsel or support. Naturally he sought support among the chief men of his realm. As the power of the Church and aristocracy increased, the king was practically forced to summon the chief persons in these classes to his Cabinet, and furthermore, in most cases, to follow their advice; so that by the close of the thirteenth century the Cabinet had become a regular institution, whose members, known as Cabinet lords, governed rather than advised the king. In the early part of the fourteenth century this institution succeeded in passing a law that each new king must summon his Cabinet immediately after his election. The same law provided that no foreigner could be a member of the Cabinet; that the archbishop should be *ex officio* a member; that twelve laymen should be summoned, but no more; and that, in addition, the king might summon as many of the bishops and clergy as he wished. As a matter of fact this law was never followed. The Cabinet lords practically formed themselves into a close corporation, appointing their own successors or compelling the king to appoint whom they desired. Generally the members were succeeded by their sons, and in very many instances we find fathers and sons sitting in the Cabinet together. A person once a Cabinet lord was such for life. The law providing that the archbishop should have a seat in the Cabinet was strictly followed, and in practice the bishops were also always members. The other clergy seem never to have been summoned except in certain instances to aid their bishops or represent them when they could not come. The provincial magistrates were generally members, though not always. As to the number of temporal lords, it was almost invariably more than twelve, sometimes double as many. From the very first, this self-appointed oligarchy saw that in unity was strength; and while the different members of the royal family were squabbling among themselves, the Cabinet seized the opportunity to increase its power. Though not entitled to a definite salary, it was regularly understood that Cabinet lords were to be paid by grants of the chief fiefs; and when these fiefs were extended so as to embrace the whole, or nearly the whole, of a province, the grant of such a fief ordinarily carried with it the office of provincial magistrate. Thus the Cabinet became the centre of administration for the kingdom. From this it gradually usurped the right to legislate for the whole realm, to lay new taxes on the people, and to negotiate treaties with foreign powers. Lastly, it robbed the people of their ancient right to nominate and confirm their kings. These prerogatives, however, were not exercised without strong opposition. Throughout the fourteenth and fifteenth centuries the peasantry battled with vigor against the arrogant assumptions of the Cabinet, never relinquishing their claim to be governed as of yore. This struggle against the encroachments of the oligarchy at last resulted in the revolution under Gustav Vasa. Hence we may with profit trace the relation between the Cabinet and the people from the start.

The first case in which the Cabinet distinctly asserted an authority over the whole land occurred in 1319, when the king, after a long and bitter struggle with different members of the royal house, had finally been driven from the throne. The Cabinet then resolved to place the crown on the head of the former monarch's grandson, a child but three years old. With this in view, they called all the magnates in the realm and four peasants from every county to a general diet, where the chancellor of the Cabinet stepped forward with the infant in his arms, and moved that this infant be elected king. "Courtiers, peasantry, and all with one accord responded, 'Amen.'" This was the first general diet held in Sweden, and it showed a marked decline in the people's rights. From beginning to end the proceedings of this diet were regulated by the Cabinet, and the people were practically forced to acquiesce. Even had the people possessed a real voice in the election, their influence would have been far less than formerly, since here they had but four representatives from each county against the entire class of magnates, whereas originally every landowner, whether magnate or peasant, had an equal vote. During the minority of this king the power of the Cabinet made rapid strides. He was forced to borrow from them enormous sums of money, for which he mortgaged nearly all the royal castles; so that when he came of age he was thoroughly under the dominion of the Cabinet. He struggled hard, however, to shake off his shackles, and with some success. Among other things, he passed a law which was intended to restore to the people at large their ancient right to choose their kings. This law provided that whenever a king was to be chosen, each provincial magistrate, with the assent of all landowners in his province, should select twelve men, who on a day appointed were to meet in general diet with all the magistrates, and choose the king. Unhappily this law was never followed, though the king by whom it was enacted struggled hard to maintain the people's rights. In 1359, after a series of internal disorders, his Cabinet compelled him to call a meeting of all the magnates in the realm; but in addition to the magnates he summoned also delegates from the peasantry and burghers, evidently with a view to gain their aid in curbing the insolence of the Cabinet. This was the second general diet. From this time forth the king did all he could to strengthen the people, until at last he banished a number of his chief opponents. They thereupon, in 1363, offered the crown to Albert of Mecklenburg, who by their aid succeeded in overthrowing the king and getting possession of the throne. For a time now the Cabinet had things nearly as they wished. In 1371 they forced the king to grant them all the royal estates as fiefs, and to declare that on the death of any one of them his successor should be chosen by the survivors. This astounding grant the Cabinet owed chiefly to the influence of their chancellor, Bo Jonsson, who had done more than any other to set Albert on the throne; and to him were granted as fiefs all the royal castles. In 1386 he died, leaving all his fiefs, by will, to the chief magnates of the land. Against this Albert ventured to protest. He called in a large number of his German countrymen, and by their aid recovered a large portion of his power. He then began distributing royal favors among them with a lavish hand, to the detriment of the Swedish magnates. These magnates therefore turned, in 1388, to Margaret, regent of Denmark and Norway, and offered her the regency of Sweden, promising to recognize as king whomever she should choose. In 1389 she entered Sweden with her army, overthrew King Albert, and got possession of the throne. In 1396 the Swedish Cabinet, at her desire, elected her nephew, Erik of Pomerania, already king of Denmark and Norway, to be king of Sweden; and on the 17th of June, 1397, he was crowned at Kalmar. Thus began the celebrated Kalmar Union, one of the greatest political blunders that a nation ever made. It was the voluntary enslavement of a whole people to suit the whims of a few disgruntled magnates.

The century following this catastrophe was marked by violence and bloodshed. In all the setting up and pulling down of kings which ended in the Kalmar Union, the Swedish peasantry, now the body of the nation, had had no part. They had long watched in silence the overpowering growth of the magnates and of the Church; they had seen their own rights gradually, but surely, undermined; and they now beheld the whole nation given into the hand of a foreign king. All this tyranny was beginning to produce its natural effect. A spirit of rebellion was spreading fast. However, open insurrection was for the moment averted by the prudence of the regent; so long as she lived the people were tolerably content. She ruled the Cabinet with an iron hand, and refused to appoint a chancellor, the officer who had hitherto done much to bind the Cabinet together. After her death Erik attempted to carry out a similar policy, and introduced a number of foreigners into the Swedish Cabinet. But his continual absence from the realm weakened his administration, and gave great license to his officers, who by their cruelty won the hatred of the people. At last, in 1433, the peasantry of Dalarne rebelled against the tyranny of the steward whom their Danish ruler had put over them, and in 1435, under the leadership of a courageous warrior, Engelbrekt Engelbrektsson, compelled the king to call a general diet, the first since 1359, consisting of all the people in the realm who cared to take part. This diet, under the enthusiasm of the moment, elected Engelbrekt commander of the kingdom. But the hopes of the peasantry were soon blasted. In the next year Engelbrekt was murdered by a Swedish magnate, and by a general diet Karl Knutsson, another magnate, was chosen to fill his place. King Erik was now tottering to his fall. He was no longer king in anything but name. His fall, however, benefited only the magnates of the realm. By a general diet of 1438, to which all people in the realm were called, Knutsson was elected regent. But his reign came in the next year to an untimely end. His fellow-magnates, jealous of his power, forced him to lay it down; and in 1440 the Cabinet called Erik's nephew, Christopher of Bavaria, already king of Denmark, to the Swedish throne. Thus ended the first effort of the Swedish peasantry to throw off the Danish yoke. It had begun with high promises for the people, but had ended in the restoration of the Cabinet to all its former power. From this time forth the Cabinet was again practically the governing body in the realm. But it was no longer at unity with itself. One party, led by the great house of Oxenstjerna, was for preserving the Union. The other consisted of the adherents of Karl Knutsson, who hoped to put the crown on his own head. In 1448 King Christopher died, and, in the difference of feeling which reigned, the Cabinet called a general diet of all the magnates with representatives from the peasantry and burghers, that the people at large might choose of the two evils that which pleased them best. The result was that Karl Knutsson was elected king. From this time till his death, in 1470, he was in perpetual warfare with the king of Denmark, with the Swedish priesthood, who had now grown fat under Danish rule and wished to continue so, and with the hostile party among the magnates. Twice he was forced to lay down the crown only to take it up again. Throughout his reign, though in some regards a despot, he was, at all events, the champion of the Swedish magnates as opposed to those who favored the continuance of foreign rule. In 1470 he died, after having intrusted Stockholm Castle to his nephew, Sten Sture. The dissension that now reigned throughout the land was great. On one side were the powerful Vasa and Oxenstjerna families, striving to put Christiern I. of Denmark on the throne. On the other side was Sten Sture, the Tott, Gyllenstjerna, Bonde, Bjelke, and Natt och Dag families, supported by the burgher element in Stockholm and the peasantry of Dalarne. With such odds on their side the issue could not long be doubtful. At a general diet held in 1471, Sten Sture was chosen regent of the kingdom. It is impossible to overrate the significance of this event. This was the first time that the burgher element played an important part in the election of Sweden's ruler. The peasantry had once before been prominent, but so long as the oligarchy held firmly together, their actual influence had been slight. Now the ranks of the oligarchy were broken. One party looked for supporters in Denmark and in the Church; the other, now gaining the upper hand, was distinctly the party of the people. The very name of regent, which was granted to Sten Sture, bears witness to the popular character of the movement. And this was destined to be the tendency of the current during the next half-century. There were many difficulties, however, with which the patriot party had to contend. In the first place, the Swedish party was in lack of funds. An enormous proportion of the kingdom was exempt from taxes, being held by magnates, who by this time claimed the right to inherit their fathers' fiefs with all the ancient privileges, but without the ancient duty to render military service. In this juncture war broke out with Russia, at the same time that the kingdom was continually harassed by Christiern, king of Denmark. It was clear that some new mode must be discovered for raising money. The peasantry were already groaning under a heavier load than they could bear. Sten therefore turned to some of the magnates, and demanded of them that they should give up a portion of their fiefs. They of course resisted, and his whole reign was occupied with a struggle to make them yield. In 1481 Christiern, king of Denmark, died, and was succeeded by his son Hans. The efforts of Sten Sture to curb the magnates had rendered him so unpopular among them, that the Swedish Cabinet now opened negotiations with the new king of Denmark. These negotiations resulted in a meeting of the Cabinets of the three Northern kingdoms, held at Kalmar in 1483. This body promulgated a decree, known in history as the Kalmar Recess, accepting Hans as king of Sweden. To this decree Sten Sture reluctantly affixed his seal. The main clauses of the decree were these: No one in Sweden was to be held accountable for past opposition to King Hans; the king was to live one year alternately in each kingdom; the high posts as well as the fiefs of Sweden should be granted to none but Swedes; and the magnates should be free to fortify their estates and refuse the king admittance. This decree, if strictly followed, would have practically freed Sweden from the yoke of Denmark. But as a matter of fact it was several years before it was destined to go into operation at all. The Swedish Cabinet were determined that no step should be taken to put the decree into effect until certain preliminary duties were discharged; among them, the cession of the island of Gotland to Sweden. These preliminaries Hans was in no hurry to perform. Meantime Sten Sture continued to act as regent. His path remained as rugged as before. Beset on all sides by enemies, each struggling for his own aggrandizement, Sten had all he could do to keep the kingdom from going to pieces. In every measure to increase the income of the crown he was hampered by the overweening power of the Cabinet, who were reluctant to give up a jot or tittle of their ill-acquired wealth. Chief among his opponents was the archbishop, Jacob Ulfsson,— a man of rare ability, but of high birth and far too fond of self-advancement. Another enemy, who ought to have been a friend, was Svante Sture, a young magnate of great talent, who first became imbittered against his illustrious namesake because the latter, on the death of Svante's father, in 1494, claimed that the fiefs which he had held should be surrendered to the crown. Of Erik Trolle, another opponent of Sten Sture, we shall see more hereafter. His strongest supporter was one Hemming Gad, a learned, eloquent, and dauntless gentleman, who also was to play a leading rôle before many years were past. In 1493 war broke out again with Russia, and Hans resolved to seize this opportunity to make good his claims in Sweden. He opened negotiations once more with the disaffected members of the Cabinet, still hoping to make compromise with Sture; they hesitated, they promised, and then made new demands; and it was in the midst of this elaborate trifling, while the regent was in Finland conducting the Russian war, that Gustav Vasa was born at Lindholm.

Affairs in Sweden were now fast coming to a crisis. The fitful struggle of a century had at last assumed a definite and unmistakable direction. All Sweden was now divided into two distinct and hostile camps, and to the dullest intellect it was clear as day that Sweden was soon to be the scene of open war. In the autumn of 1496 the Cabinet, seeing that Sture was thoroughly determined to check their power, resolved to hesitate no longer. They therefore despatched a messenger to Hans, inviting him to a congress of the three realms to be held at midsummer of the following year, when, as they gave him reason to expect, the Kalmar Recess should be put into effect. This news being brought to Sture in Finland, he set forth post-haste for Sweden, and called a meeting of the Cabinet. The members failed to appear on the day appointed, and when at last they came, they were accompanied by a large body of armed retainers. At a session held in Stockholm on the 7th of March, the Cabinet declared Sture deposed, assigning as reasons, first, that he had mismanaged the war with Russia, and, secondly, that he had maltreated certain of the Swedish magnates. The regent waited two days before making a reply, and then informed the Cabinet that, as he had been appointed to the regency by joint action of the Cabinet and people, he felt bound to hold it till requested by the same powers to lay it down. The Cabinet had nothing for it but to acquiesce, and letters were issued summoning a general diet. That diet, however, was never held. On the very day when the Cabinet made its armistice with Sture, Hans put forth a declaration of war, and at once proceeded with his fleet to Kalmar. The enemies of Sture now openly embraced the Danish cause; and the regent was forced to go to Dalarne, to get together a force with which to defend the kingdom. Here he was received with enthusiasm by the people, who saw in him the defender of their rights. At the head of a detachment of Dalesmen, reinforced by his army now recalled from Finland, he marched to Upsala, and laid siege to the archbishop's palace. By the middle of July it fell; and Sture advanced to Stäket, a strongly fortified castle of the archbishop, about thirty miles south of Upsala. While beleaguering this place, he learned that a portion of the Danish forces were advancing on the capital. He therefore relinquished the siege of Stäket, and proceeded to Stockholm, where he held himself in readiness to repel the enemy. On the 29th of September, being led by a ruse outside the city, he was surrounded by the Danes, and was able to recover the castle only after heavy loss. This battle sealed his fate. Finding himself far outnumbered, he deemed it wise to yield; and on the 6th of October, 1497, Hans was recognized by him as king.

The reign of Hans lasted about four years. At first he appeared desirous to promote the welfare of Sweden and to conform to the terms of the Kalmar Recess. But before long even the Cabinet began to grow weary of their king. The benefits conferred upon them were not so great as they had hoped. As for Sture, at his renunciation of the regency he had been granted extensive fiefs both in Sweden and in Finland; but in 1499 the king forced him to resign a large portion of these fiefs. The other members of the Cabinet, now having less cause of jealousy, became more friendly to Sten Sture. His old enemy, Svante Sture, was at length reconciled to him through the mediation of their common admirer, Dr. Hemming Gad. Even with the clergy Sten Sture was now on better terms; and at his solicitation, in January, 1501, the Chapter of Linköping elected Gad to fill their vacant see. The main ground of complaint against Hans was that he disregarded the clause of the Recess which forbade the granting of Swedish fiefs to Danes. Matters reached a crisis in 1501, when Sten and Svante Sture, Gad, and three others met in council and took oath to resist the oppression of their foreign ruler. This step was the signal for a general explosion. On every side the people rose in arms. Hans was in despair. He first took counsel with his warm supporter, the archbishop, and then, on the 11th of August, 1501, set off with his whole fleet for Denmark.

In the royal castle at Stockholm he left his wife Christina, who, with Erik Trolle and a force of one thousand men, was determined to resist. Gad, whose election to the bishopric of Linköping the pope refused to ratify, undertook to besiege the castle. Meantime Svante Sture laid siege to Örebro, and Sten proceeded to Dalarne and other parts to gather forces. On the 12th of November the Cabinet again called Sten Sture to the regency. In February the Castle of Örebro fell. And still Christina with her brave followers held out. Not till the 9th of May, after a bloody assault, could the patriots force a passage. Then they found that, of the one thousand who had formed the original garrison, but seventy were alive. Christina was conveyed to Vadstena, where she remained several months pending negotiations. At the close of the year 1503 she was accompanied to the frontier by the regent, who however was taken ill on his return journey, and died at Jönköping on the 13th of December, 1503. Sten Sture had done much for Sweden. Though himself a magnate, and ambitious to increase his power, he was zealous for the welfare of his country, and did more than any other of his time to awake Sweden to a sense of her existence as a nation. It was on the foundation laid by him that a still greater leader was soon to build a mighty edifice.

On the 21st of January, 1504, at a general diet of the magnates, with delegates from the burghers and peasantry of Sweden, Svante Sture was elected regent. His reign was even more warlike than that of his predecessor. The Cabinet, it is true, had come to see the benefits resulting from Sten Sture's rule, and the majority of them were lukewarm adherents of the Swedish party. But Hans was more determined than ever to seize the crown, and not only harassed Svante throughout his reign by a long series of invasions, but did all he could to compromise him with other foreign powers. Svante, however, succeeded in winning many friends. In 1504 he concluded a truce of twenty years with Russia, which was extended, by treaty of 1510, to 1564. In 1510 an alliance was also formed between Sweden and the Vend cities. In 1506 the Dalesmen, at one of their assemblies, issued a letter to the people of their provinces, urging them to support Svante with life and limb. But this burst of enthusiasm was short-lived. The war with Hans hung on. New taxes had to be imposed, and several fiefs to which different magnates laid claim were appropriated to the crown. Discontent spread once more, and at a Cabinet meeting held in September, 1511, Svante was declared deposed. He refused to yield till heard by a general diet of the kingdom, and while negotiations were pending, on the 2d of January, 1512, he died.

Nothing could have given certain members of the Cabinet greater pleasure. The clerical members especially, being warmly attached to the Danish cause, thought they now saw an opportunity to set Hans on the throne. About the middle of January the Cabinet came together and, at the solicitation of Archbishop Ulfsson, resolved to intrust the government for the time being to Erik Trolle. This gentleman, of whom we have already seen something, was of high birth as well as talent, thoroughly versed in affairs, and allied to the Danish party not only by family connection, but also by reason of large estates in Denmark. He was, moreover, a warm friend of the archbishop.

However, the hopes of Trolle were not destined to be realized. At the death of Svante, the Castle of Örebro was in command of a daring and ambitious youth of nineteen, known to history as Sten Sture the Younger. He was Svante's son, and in the preceding year had married Christina Gyllenstjerna, a great-granddaughter of King Karl Knutsson. Immediately on hearing of his father's death, he hastened to Vesterås, took possession of the castle, and despatched a messenger to convey the news to Stockholm. On the 8th of January the steward of Stockholm Castle declared his readiness to yield the command to Sture, and within a day or two the castles of Stegeborg and Kalmar were also given up. The energy with which this chivalrous youth seized the helm is all the more astounding when we reflect that he stood almost alone against the Cabinet. He could not even ask the advice of Gad, his father's trusty friend, for that doughty patriot was at the moment outside the realm. But his zeal won him numerous friends among the younger magnates, and the peasantry throughout the country were on his side. All winter long the battle raged between the two factions, but meantime Sture continually grew in favor. No general diet of the kingdom was summoned, but it was understood on every hand that the matter would be submitted to the people when they came together on St. Erik's day at Upsala. On that day, May 18, the archbishop and his followers addressed the people in the Grand Square at Upsala, and announced that the Cabinet had resolved to raise Erik Trolle to the regency. But they were met by shouts from the crowd, who declared that they would have no Danes. Meantime Sture had been holding a mass-meeting on the so-called Royal Meadow outside the town, and had been enthusiastically applauded by the people. Even yet, however, the conflict did not cease. The Cabinet still clamored for Erik Trolle, and it was not till the 23d of July, when every hope was gone, that they finally gave way and recognized Sture as regent. Sture now set forth on a journey through Sweden and Finland, receiving everywhere the allegiance of the people. All at last seemed in his favor, when suddenly, on the 20th of February, 1513, the face of things was changed by the unexpected death of Hans.

Before considering the effect of this catastrophe, let us return to the little boy whom we last saw on his father's estate at Rydboholm. Even he was not wholly outside the conflict. His father, Erik, whom we find in 1488 subscribing his name as a knight, took an active part in the commotions of his times, and early won ill-favor with King Hans. The young Gustav in his fifth year, so runs the story, happened to be playing in the hall of Stockholm Castle, when King Hans espied him, and, attracted by his winning manners, patted him on the head and said, "You'll be a great man in your day, if you live." But when he found out who the child was, he wanted to carry him off to Denmark with him. To this the boy's great-uncle, Sture, raised serious objections, and lest the king should use some treachery, hurried Gustav out of the way at once. In the very next year, 1501, occurred the rebellion against Hans, which resulted in the election of Sture to the regency. Erik was one of the supporters of his uncle throughout this strife, and in 1502 we find him signing a document as member of the Cabinet. About the same time he was made commandant of Kastelholm Castle. This post, however, he held but a short time, and then retired to his old estate at Rydboholm. Among his children, besides Gustav, were one younger boy, Magnus, and several girls. Gustav, we are told, was a handsome, attractive little fellow, and it is added that in his sports he was always recognized as leader by his playmates. In 1509, when in his thirteenth year, he was sent by his parents to Upsala, and placed in a preparatory school. Soon after, probably in the next year, Gustav was admitted to the University. This institution, which had been founded in 1477, through the persistent efforts of Archbishop Ulfsson, and of which the archbishop was chancellor, was at this time in a semi-dormant state. Scarce anything is known either about its professors or about the number of its students. It is probable, however, that Peder Galle, who was cantor of the Upsala Chapter so early as 1504, and whose powers as a theological gladiator will become known to us further on, was one of the professors. Another was Henrik Sledorn, whom Gustav later made his chancellor. Of the progress made by Gustav in his studies we know nothing. It may well be surmised, however, that the politics of his day engrossed a large share of his attention. Upsala was not then the peaceful town that it now is, and the chancellor of the University was in the very vortex of the struggle. If Gustav was still connected with the University in 1512, we may suppose with reason that he took his part in the great demonstration which resulted in the election of the chivalric young Sture.

FIRST MILITARY ADVENTURES OF GUSTAV; A PRISONER IN DENMARK. 1514-1519.

THE old town of Stockholm was beyond all doubt the most picturesque capital in Europe. Perched on an isle of rock at the eastern extremity of Lake Mälar, it stood forth like a sentinel guarding the entrance to the heart of Sweden. Around its base on north and south dashed the foaming waters of the Mälar, seeking their outlet through a narrow winding channel to the Baltic. Across this channel on the south, and connected with the city by a bridge, the towering cliffs of Södermalm gazed calmly down upon the busy traffic of the city's streets; and far away beyond the channel on the north stretched an undulating plain, dotted with little patches of green shrubbery and forest. On the west the city commanded a wide view over an enchanting lake studded with darkly wooded isles, above whose trees peeped here and there some grim turret or lofty spire. Finally, in the east, the burgher standing on the city's walls could trace for several miles the current of a silver stream, glittering in the sunlight, and twisting in and out among the islands along the coast until at last it lost itself in the mighty waters of the Baltic.

The town itself was small. The main isle, on which "the city," so called, was built, stretched scarce a quarter of a mile from east to west and but little more from north to south. Nestling under the shadow of the main isle were two smaller isles, Riddarholm on the west and Helgeandsholm on the north, both severed from the city by a channel about fifty feet in width. Through the centre of the main isle ran a huge backbone of rock, beginning at the south and rising steadily till within a few feet of the northern shore. The summit of this ridge was crowned by the royal citadel, a massive edifice of stone, the northern wall of which ran close along the shore, so that the soldier on patrol could hear the ripple of the water on the rocks below. From either side of the citadel the town walls ran south at a distance of perhaps a hundred feet from the shore, meeting at a point about the same distance from the southern channel. Within the triangle thus formed, not over twenty-five acres all told, lived and moved five thousand human beings. The streets, it need scarce be said, were narrow, dark, and damp. The houses were lofty, generally with high pitch-roofs to prevent the snow from gathering on them. The doors and windows were high, but narrow to keep out the cold, and were built in the sides of the house, not in front, owing to the darkness and narrowness of the streets. To economize space, most of the houses were built in blocks of five or six, wholly separated from their neighbors and forming a sort of castle by themselves. The only church inside the walls was the so-called Great Church on the summit of the hill. Adjoining this church on the south was the old town-hall. As to public squares, there were but two,—the Grand Square, on the summit of the hill immediately south of the town-hall; and the so-called Iron Market, a smaller square just inside the southern gate. These squares, the largest not more than eighty yards in length, served at once as the market, the promenade, and the place of execution for the town. The town-walls were fortified at several points by towers, and were entered by gateways at the northwest corner and at the southern point, as well as by several small gateways along the sides. The city was connected with the mainland north and south by turreted bridges, the north bridge passing across the island of Helgeandsholm. All around the main island, some fifty feet from the shore, ran a long bridge on piles, built as a safeguard against hostile ships. Protected thus by nature and by art from foreign intrusion, the burghers of Stockholm learned to rely on their own industry and skill for every need. They formed themselves into various trades or guilds, each under the surveillance of a master. To be admitted to a guild it was necessary to pass a severe examination in the particular trade. These guilds were marked by an intense *esprit de corps*, each striving to excel the others in display of wealth. Some guilds were composed wholly of tradespeople, others wholly of artisans; and there were still others formed for social or religious purposes, comprising members of various trades. Of these latter guilds the most aristocratic and influential was the Guild of the Sacred Body. Inside a guild the members were bound together by the warmest bonds of friendship. They ordinarily lived in the same quarter of the town; they cared for their brothers in sickness or poverty, and said Mass in common for the souls of their deceased. Each guild held meetings at stated intervals to vote on various matters concerning its affairs. In case of war the different guilds enlisted in separate companies. Over and above all the guilds were a burgomaster and council elected by their fellow-townsmen, their duties being to regulate the relations of the various guilds to one another, and provide for the general welfare of the city. Thus the inhabitants of Stockholm formed a miniature republic by themselves. They governed themselves in nearly all local matters. They bought, sold, and exchanged according to their own laws and regulations. They married and gave in marriage after their own caprice. Industrious, skilful, with little ambition, they bustled about their narrow streets, jostling those at their elbow and uttering slander against those out of hearing. In short, they led the humdrum life incident to all small towns in time of peace, and were ever eager to vary this monotony at the first sound of war.

Into this community Gustav was ushered in the year 1514. He was then but eighteen, and was summoned by the regent to the royal court to complete his education. He found himself at once in clover. Three years before, his mother's half-sister, Christina Gyllenstjerna, had married the young regent; and the youth on coming to Stockholm was received as one of the family in the royal palace.

Among all the personages then at court, the most interesting, by all odds, was the regent's wife, Christina. This woman is one of the most puzzling characters in Swedish history. On her father's side of royal lineage, and on her mother's descended from one of the oldest families in Sweden, she inherited at the same time a burning desire for personal advancement and an enthusiasm for the glory of her native land. Wedded to a handsome, daring, impetuous youth of twenty-one, the nation's favorite, she entered with her whole heart into all his projects, and was among his most valuable counsellors whether in peace or war. In force of character and in personal bravery she was scarce inferior to her heroic husband, and yet she lacked not discretion or even shrewdness. She was the idol of the Swedish people, and before many years were passed was to have an opportunity to test their love.

Another personage at court, with whom we have already become acquainted, was Hemming Gad. Although of humble birth, this man had received a careful education, and during twenty years of his early life had held the post of Swedish ambassador at the court of Rome. On his return to Sweden he had been elected bishop of the diocese of Linköping, but had never entered on his duties owing to the opposition of the pope. He was not indeed a priest. Diplomacy was above all else the field in which he shone. A warm supporter of the Stures, he had more than once averted trouble by his powers of conciliation, and was regarded as an indispensable servant of the people's cause. Fearless, eloquent, untiring, conciliatory, persuasive, perhaps not too conscientious, he was the most influential person in the Cabinet and one of the very foremost statesmen of his time. It was to this man, then seventy-four years of age, that the care of the young Gustav was intrusted when he came to court.

Affairs at this time were in a state of great confusion. King Hans of Denmark had died a year before, and after several months of hostile demonstration had been succeeded by his son. This person, known as Christiern II., was as vile a monster as ever occupied a throne. Gifted by nature with a powerful frame, tall, burly, with large head and short thick neck, broad forehead and high cheek-bones, prominent nose, firmly compressed lips, a plentiful supply of shaggy hair on his head and face, heavy overhanging eyebrows, his eyes small, deep-set, and fierce,—his appearance furnished an excellent index to his character. Firm, courageous, by no means wanting in intellect or executive ability, he was sensual, gross, and cruel. Though often full of hilarity and hearty animal spirits, there was ever hanging over him a cloud of melancholy, which occasionally settled on him with such weight as to rob him wholly of his reason. At such times he seemed transformed into some fierce monster with an insatiable thirst for blood. When a mere boy in the royal palace at Copenhagen, he is said to have amused himself by midnight orgies about the city's streets. He was well educated, however, and early became a useful adjunct to his father. At twenty-one he displayed much bravery in an assault which Hans then made on Stockholm; and a few years later he became his father's deputy in the government of Norway. While there, his secretary one day came to him and portrayed in glowing terms the beauty of a maiden who had dazzled him in Bergen. The sensitive heart of Christiern at once was fired. He left his castle at Opslo without a moment's waiting, and, crossing hill and vale without a murmur, hastened to feast his eyes on the fair Dyveke. Being of a romantic turn of mind, he resolved to see her first amidst all the fashion of the town. A splendid ball was therefore held, to which the aristocracy were bidden with their daughters. Among the guests was the renowned Dyveke, who outshone all in beauty. No sooner did Christiern see her, than his whole soul burned within him. He seized her hand, and led off the dance in company with his fair enchanter. Rapture filled his soul; and when the ball was over, Dyveke was secretly detained and brought to Christiern's bed. This incident had a far-reaching influence on Christiern's later life. Though already betrothed to the sister of Charles V., his passion for Dyveke did not pass away. He erected a palace at Opslo, and lived there with his mistress until recalled to Copenhagen, when he took her with him. The most singular feature in this whole intrigue is that the royal voluptuary was from the outset under the absolute sway, not of the fair Dyveke, but of her mother, Sigbrit, a low, cunning, intriguing woman of Dutch origin, who followed the couple to the royal palace at Opslo, and afterwards accompanied them to Stockholm, the complete ruler of her daughter's royal slave. On the accession of Christiern to the throne, he resolved, at the instance of this woman, to add the Swedish kingdom to his dominions. In order to comprehend the measures which he adopted, it will be necessary to trace events in Sweden since the death of Hans.

The Danish party, in no way daunted by their futile effort to secure the regency of Sweden, had kept up continuous negotiations with their friends in Denmark, with the object ultimately to place the king of Denmark on the throne. Owing, however, to the manifest and growing popularity of the young Sture, they deemed it wise to wait for a more auspicious moment before making open demonstration, and for the time being yielded to the regent with the best grace they could command. The thing which they most needed, in order to counteract the influence of the chivalric young Sture, was the infusion of new life among their ranks. The archbishop and Erik Trolle both were old, and, though in the full vigor of their intellectual ability, lacked the energy and endurance required to carry on a policy of active war. It was resolved, therefore, to throw the burden of leadership on younger shoulders. There was at this time in Rome a man who seemed to possess more qualifications than any other for the post. This was Gustaf Trolle. He was young, highly educated, energetic, and above all a son of Erik Trolle, the powerful leader of the Danish faction. He had seen much of the world, and had lived on terms of familiarity with some of the greatest men in Europe. But his whole power of usefulness was lost through his inordinate personal and family pride. Weighted down by the sense of his own importance, with haughty overbearing manners, and a dogged obstinacy in dealing with his inferiors, he was the last man in the world to be successful as a party leader. Yet it was on this man that the Danish party fixed its hopes. The matter first took shape on the 31st of August, 1514, when the archbishop in conversation with Sture suggested that old age was now coming on so fast that he desired to resign his office, and asked whom Sture deemed most fit to serve as his successor. To this the courteous regent answered that he knew no one better fitted for the post than the archbishop himself. With this the conversation ended. On the 12th of October following, the crafty archbishop, not averse to feathering his own nest, formed a compact with Erik Trolle by which Ulfsson was to commend the latter's son for the archbishopric, and in return Erik promised to support Ulfsson to the utmost of his power and to see that Gustaf Trolle did not deprive Ulfsson of the archiepiscopal rents during the latter's life. This done, Erik Trolle went to the regent and asked him to recommend Gustaf Trolle for the post of archdeacon of Upsala. This request was complied with. But when, soon after, Erik appeared again before the regent with a letter from the archbishop informing him that the Chapter of Upsala had decided on Gustaf Trolle as the new archbishop, Sture was so startled that he wrote to Upsala to say that he had never consented to such a proposition, but nevertheless if God wished it he would raise no opposition. The pope having already declared that no one should be appointed without the regent's consent, no effort was spared to dispose Sture well towards the new candidate, and with so good result that when the archbishop's messengers went to Rome to secure the confirmation, they carried with them a letter from Sture to his legate in Rome, instructing him to do all he could before the pope in favor of Gustaf Trolle.

In May, 1515, the young man was consecrated archbishop of Upsala by the pope, and started in the following summer for the North. Passing through Lubeck, where he is rumored to have had an audience of Christiern, he pursued his journey by water, and at last cast anchor off the Swedish coast about twelve miles from Stockholm. Here he was met by certain of the Danish party, who urged him to give the cold shoulder to the regent. Instead, therefore, of proceeding to the capital, he drove direct to Upsala, and was installed in his new office: all this in spite of the fact that the old archbishop had assured the regent, before he wrote to Rome, that he would not hand over Upsala nor Stäket to Trolle till the latter had sworn allegiance to Sture. The immediate effect of his investiture was to augment the haughtiness of the young archbishop. Scarcely had he become domiciled in Upsala, when he wrote a letter to the regent warning him that he, the archbishop, was about to visit with punishment all who had wronged his father or grandfather, or his predecessor in the archiepiscopal chair. To this the regent, wishing if possible to avert trouble, answered that if any persons had done the wrong complained of, he would see to it that they should be punished. But the archbishop was in no mood for compromise. The breach now opened, he resolved to make it wider; and he had no difficulty in finding pretext. The fief of Stäket had long been a bone of contention between the Church and State. Though for many years in the hands of the archbishops, it had never been clearly settled whether they held it as a right or merely by courtesy of the crown; and at the resignation of Archbishop Ulfsson the fief was claimed by his successor, Trolle, as well as by the regent. In order to put an end to this vexed question, the regent wrote to Ulfsson asking him to produce the title-deeds on which his claim was based. After considerable correspondence, in which, however, the deeds were not produced, Sture, deeming it unwise to leave the fief any longer without a steward, entered into possession, and applied the incomes to the royal treasury, at the same time assuring Ulfsson that if he or the Chapter at Upsala could prove a title to the fief, they should enjoy it. This only added fuel to the flame. Trolle, unable as it seems to prove his title, assumed the posture of one who had been wronged, and scorned the urgent invitation of the regent to come to Stockholm and discuss the matter. Indeed, there were rumors in the air to the effect that Trolle was engaged in a conspiracy against the throne.

letter from King Christiern promising all who gave their aid in establishing him on the throne a double recompense for any loss incurred in the attempt. No time was, therefore, to be lost. Collecting a force with all haste from different parts of Sweden, the regent advanced on Stäket to besiege the castle. Immediately on their arrival, Trolle sent out word that he desired a parley. This was granted, and the archbishop came outside the walls to a spot before the Swedish camp. In the course of the discussion, Trolle, perhaps with a view to intimidate the regent, declared that he had within the castle a letter from King Christiern announcing that he would come to the relief before the 1st of May. But the young regent was not so easily to be intimidated. His terms were that Trolle and his men might withdraw unharmed from Stäket, and that the archbishop might continue in possession of the Cathedral of Upsala and all the privileges of his office; but that the Castle of Stäket, long a prolific source of discord, should remain in the hands of Sture till a tribunal composed of clergy as well as laity could determine whether it should belong to Church or State, or be demolished as a source of discord. These terms were not accepted, and the siege continued. All through the winter and spring the Swedish army bivouacked outside the walls; and Trolle, ever looking for aid from Denmark, refused to yield. At last, at midsummer, having received tidings that rescue was near at hand, his heart grew bold within him, and he resolved to make a dupe of Sture. The latter not being at the time at Stäket, the archbishop sent a messenger to say that he was ready for a parley. The regent, daily fearing the approach of Christiern, received the messenger with joy. He called together the burgomaster and Council of Stockholm, and instructed them to select delegates to act in behalf of Stockholm. With these delegates and a few advisers on his own account he proceeded to Stäket, and after consultation as to the terms which they should offer, signalled the guard on the castle walls that he was ready to treat with Trolle. After standing some time in the midst of a pouring rain, and without any prospect of an answer, the regent grew impatient, and sent word to Trolle that he could offer no other terms than those already offered. The charlatan then threw off the mask. He replied that he placed implicit confidence in Christiern, and was in no hurry for a parley. Any time within six weeks would do. At this announcement the regent had nothing for it but to withdraw. Drenched to the skin, and burning at the insult offered him, he returned to Stockholm.

He did so none too soon. The Danish forces, four thousand strong, were already off the Swedish coast. This was by no means the first proof of actual hostilities on the part of Christiern. Six months before, while the truce between the kingdoms was still in force, Christiern had seized a Swedish vessel while lying in the roads outside Lubeck, and at the general diet held at New Year's in Arboga, it had been voted to resist the tyrant till the dying breath. As a result, the congress of the three realms which was to have been held in February had never met. A broadside was issued by the regent to all the men of Sweden, calling on them to prepare for war. Throughout the spring and summer the advent of the tyrant was expected, and the announcement that his army had at length arrived was a surprise to none.

It was early in the month of August, 1517, when the Danish fleet was sighted off the coast twelve miles from Stockholm. Sture proceeded at once to the point at which it was expected they would land, and thus prevented them. The fleet hovered about the coast for several days, sending out pillaging parties in small boats to the shore. One of these parties was intercepted; and from a prisoner who was taken, Sture learned definitely that the object of the expedition was to go to the relief of Stäket. On this news Sture sent some members of the Cabinet to Stäket to inform the archbishop that the Danish force was now off Stockholm, and to urge him in behalf of the town of Stockholm to send word to the Danish force that it could count on no aid from him, as he was resolved to remain true to his native land. But this final appeal to the archbishop's honor met with no response. The fleet meantime had approached the capital, and was riding at anchor about two miles down the stream. There the whole force landed, intending to march direct to Stäket. But the young regent was again ahead of them. Scarce had they set foot on shore when he fell upon them with his army. The conflict was sharp and bitter, but at last the regent came off victorious. The Danes were driven headlong to their ships, leaving many of their number dead upon the shore, while others fell captives into the hand of Sture. This was a red-letter day in the calendar of the regent, and is specially memorable as being the first occasion on which the young Gustav drew sword in behalf of his native land.

Elated by his victory, the regent now opened communications once more with Trolle. With a view to frighten him into submission, he sent some of the Danish captives to Stäket, that the archbishop might hear from his own allies the story of their disaster. Even at this the proud spirit of the archbishop was not humbled. He still persisted in his determination not to yield, and it was only when his own officers began to leave him that he signified his willingness to withdraw from Stäket and retire to the duties of his cathedral. But now it was Sture's turn to dictate. He answered curtly that a murderer could no longer be archbishop, and proceeded at once to summon a general diet of the kingdom. This diet met at Stockholm in the last days of November. It was a notable gathering. Among those present were four of the six bishops,—all except the bishops of Vexiö and Skara,—of laymen, Hemming Gad and the father of young Gustav, besides some ten other knights and armigers, the burgomaster and Council of Stockholm, and a large number of delegates from the peasantry. Before this assembly the archbishop appeared, under safe-conduct from the regent, to plead his cause. Among the witnesses produced in favor of the crown was a Danish officer captured in the battle outside Stockholm. This man testified, among other things, that before the Danish fleet set forth, a messenger from Trolle had appeared before King Christiern to solicit aid for Stäket. Indeed, the charge of conspiracy was proved beyond the shadow of a doubt. The whole house rose with one accord in denunciation of the traitor. Without a dissenting voice it was decreed that Stäket, "the rebel stronghold," should be levelled to the ground; that Trolle should nevermore be recognized as archbishop; that, though by the terms of his safe-conduct he might return to Stäket, he should not come forth therefrom till he had given pledge to do no further injury to the kingdom; and, finally, that if Trolle or any other in his behalf should solicit excommunication on any of those present for this resolve or for besieging or destroying Stäket, or should otherwise molest them, they all should stand firm by one another. This resolve, before the diet parted, was put into writing, and to it every member attached his seal.

The archbishop, as had been promised him, was permitted to return to Stäket, which was again put into a state of siege. The siege, however, was of short duration. Deserted by the largest portion of his officers, and with no immediate prospect of further aid from Denmark, the archbishop had nothing for it but to yield. Stäket thus fell into the hands of Sture; and the archbishop was placed in the monastery of Vesterås, to remain there captive till further disposition should be made of his archbishopric.

The whole country was by this time overrun with rebels. Particularly along the southern frontier the Danish party, in close alliance with the king of Denmark, kept the inhabitants in a state of terror; and their hostile demonstrations became at last so marked that the regent found it necessary, in the autumn of 1517, to despatch his army thither to repress them. This news was brought to Christiern's ears, still tingling with the report of the disaster of his fleet. The monarch, having no stomach for a winter campaign among the snows of Sweden, bethought him of a truce until the coming spring. There chanced to be in Denmark at the time a smooth-mouthed scoundrel with the unsavory name of Arcimboldo. He was by trade a dealer in indulgences, having been commissioned by Leo X. to vend his wares throughout the northern parts of Europe. He had already spent some time in Lubeck, where he had reaped a splendid harvest; and had now been carrying on his business about two years in Denmark. On every church he had affixed a chest with notice that all who would contribute to the sacred cause should receive full absolution from their sins. It certainly was a tempting offer, and one which the unwary believers in the papal authority were not slow to seize. They poured in their contributions with a lavish hand, and the legate soon amassed a princely fortune. At last, however, his goods began to be a drug upon the market, and he prepared to transfer his headquarters to another land. It was about this time, early in the winter of 1518, that Christiern made up his mind to suggest a truce with Sweden, and the grand idea occurred to him of enlisting the papal legate in his service. He summoned the pardon-monger without delay, and suggested that he should mediate with Sture. To this suggestion Arcimboldo, by no means averse to turning an honest penny, gave his assent. He sat down at once and wrote a letter to the regent, instructing him that the pope desired to see peace made between the kingdoms. He therefore, as ambassador from his Holiness, suggested that Sture should observe a truce by land with Denmark till the 23d of April next, and in the mean time should send delegates to the town of Lund with full power to make a lasting peace between the kingdoms. To this proposal the legate added that Christiern had given his consent. This document was handed to the regent about the middle of February. He sent back a despatch at once, thanking the legate for his efforts in behalf of peace, and expressing a wish to accede in general to the proposition. It would not be possible, however, to send delegates to a congress on so short a notice. Before doing so it would be necessary to hold a general diet, so that the people of Sweden might vote upon the matter; and as some of the members would have to come from Finland, the diet could not be held unless the truce was extended so as to embrace the sea. But he should be pleased if Arcimboldo would effect a lasting treaty between the kingdoms, or even a truce by sea and land to continue for the life of Christiern. He, on his part, would summon a general diet as soon as possible, with a view to bring about a lasting peace. Thus the peace negotiations came to naught. Christiern had no intention of consenting to a lasting peace, and Sture was not to be inveigled into a truce which had no other object than to give the king of Denmark an opportunity to recruit.

And thus the winter wore away, and spring came, and both parties were gathering up their forces to renew the war. In the little town of Stockholm a spirit of patriotism was growing fast. It was felt on every hand that the coming summer would forever settle the question of slavery or freedom, and all were fixed in purpose to resist the tyrant till their dying breath. Children, from fifteen upwards, were in arms, momentarily expecting the arrival of the Danish fleet. But the agony was prolonged day after day till the sturdy patriots were eager to have it close. Excitement had been wrought up to a fever heat, when, in the month of June, the news was shouted through the narrow streets that the enemy's vessels were at hand. The report was true. There in the stream below the town were visible the white sails of the Danish squadron,— eighty ships in all,—slowly forging their way against the current towards the town. It was a sight to make even the stout heart of a Stockholm burgher quail. The fleet approached within a short distance, and the troops were landed on the southern shore, separated from the city only by a narrow channel. The Danish king himself was in command. His forces consisted of five thousand Germans, besides a thousand light-armed soldiers chiefly Danes, a hundred horse, and a vast multitude of laborers for building dikes and trenches. Proceeding to the west, he took up his position, June 29, on the hill opposite the city on the north. But he soon discovered that this point was too far from the town. He therefore crossed over to the southern shore, and pitched his camp on the cliffs of Södermalm. From this point he began to bombard the tower at the southern corner of the town. After battering this tower near a month, he sent a force across the bridge with orders to burst through the wall at the point which his guns had shaken. The effort, however, was of no avail. His force was driven back and compelled to seek safety beyond the bridge. At this juncture news arrived that a detachment of the Swedish army was coming against him on the south. Fearing a simultaneous attack on both sides, he hastily advanced in the direction of the expected onslaught, and threw up a fortification at Brännkyrka, about three miles south of Stockholm. On his right the land was boggy and overgrown with brushwood, while on his left it was somewhat higher and wooded. In these woods the Swedish army gathered. It is reported that they were twelve thousand strong, but they consisted chiefly of ill-trained and ill-armed peasants. The regent had joined them, and was leading them in person. The royal banners of the first battalion were in charge of Gustav Vasa. After a few days' skirmishing, in which the patriots were twice driven into the covert of their woods, the Danes made a final charge upon them, and put them once more to flight. This time, however, the Danish soldiers lost their heads, and followed in hot haste through the forest. In this way they lost all advantage from their superior arms and training. The Swedes, nearly twice as numerous as their opponents, surrounded them, and closed in upon them on every side. The forest was soon red with blood. The patriots fought with vigor and determination; and at length, though sixteen hundred of their companions were stretched upon the ground, the day was theirs. Sture collected his men as quickly as possible and returned to Stockholm, while Christiern took up his quarters again in Södermalm. A few days later Christiern, his powder and provisions failing him, ordered a retreat; but before his men were all embarked the Swedes were on them, and killed or captured some two hundred on the shore. After proceeding down the stream about twelve miles, the fleet cast anchor near the northern shore, and a foraging party was sent out towards Upsala for provisions. Some of these were captured, but the majority returned with a rich booty to their ships. Nearly two months had now elapsed since the arrival of the Danish fleet, and the cold weather was approaching. Christiern, worsted at every point, was eager to return to Denmark. But the equinoctial storm would soon be coming, and he was afraid to venture out in rough weather on short rations. His men too, suffering for food and clamoring for their pay, began to leave him. He therefore resolved to play upon another string. On the 28th of August he despatched envoys to the regent with the preposterous proposition that he should be received as king, or that in lieu thereof he should receive from the regent and Cabinet of Sweden a yearly stipend, and that the losses which he and the Danish party in Sweden had suffered should be repaid them. This ridiculous offer was of course rejected. Christiern then came down from his high horse, and proposed a cessation of hostilities till the difficulty could be settled. After some bickering on both sides it was agreed that a congress of the three realms should meet on the 10th of the following July, to determine Christiern's right to the crown of Sweden or to tribute; and until that day there should be peace between the realms. This agreement was put into writing and signed and sealed by Christiern and the regent a few days before September 8. The regent then ordered provisions sent out to the Danish soldiers to relieve their want. And still the fleet continued to hang about the coast, waiting, so it was given out, for fair weather. In reality, the Danish monarch was dallying with the hope of putting into effect a diabolical scheme which he had concocted. There being now a truce between the kingdoms, he ventured to despatch a messenger to Sture with hostages, to beg the regent to come out to the fleet and hold a conference. After consultation with his Cabinet, the regent answered that he could not accede to this request, and the hostages were returned. Christiern then sent again to say that he would gladly meet him at an appointed spot on land, provided six persons named—among them Hemming Gad and the regent's nephew, Gustav—should first be placed on board the Danish fleet as hostages. A day was set and the hostages set forth. All unconscious, the rope was already tightening around their necks. On the 25th of September, as had been agreed, the regent rode to the appointed place of meeting. But the Danish king was nowhere to be seen. Two whole days the regent waited, and on the third discovered that he had been entrapped. The fleet was on its way to Denmark, and the Swedish hostages were prisoners on board. Before putting out to sea, the monarch touched land once more to despatch a couple of letters,—one to the burghers of Stockholm, the other to all the inhabitants of Sweden. These letters are dated October 2. Their purpose was to make his treachery seem less brutal. He declared that the regent had violated the terms of the truce by ill-treating the Danish prisoners in his hands, and not surrendering them as had been stipulated in the treaty. "On this ground," said the tyrant, some four days after seizing the hostages, "I declare the treaty off."

Repairing with his captives to Copenhagen, the tyrant placed them in confinement in different parts of Denmark. Gustav was placed in Kalö Castle, under the charge of the commandant, who was a distant relative of the young man's mother. The commandant was under bonds for the safe-keeping of his prisoner; but being a man of tender feelings, he imposed little restraint upon Gustav, merely exacting from him a promise that he would make no effort to escape. His life therefore was, to outward appearance, not devoid of pleasure. The castle was situated on a promontory in Jutland, at the northern end of Kalö Bay. Its wall ran close along the cliffs, a hundred feet above the sea. At either end of the castle was a gray stone tower, and from the windows in the towers was a charming prospect on every side. The promontory was connected with the mainland by a low and narrow strip of land, and along the main shore ran a dense forest belonging to the castle and plentifully stocked with game. All these pleasures were at the free disposal of the captive. But there was a canker ever gnawing at his heart. No matter which way he turned, he heard only rumors of fresh preparations to conquer Sweden. When guests visited the castle, they talked from morn till night of the splendid armaments of Christiern. On one occasion he heard them declare that so soon as Sweden fell, her aristocracy were to be put to the sword and their wives and daughters parted out among the peasantry of Denmark. The Swedish peasants, they said, would soon learn to drive the plough with one arm and a wooden leg. Such jests made the young prisoner burn with indignation. He felt it necessary to conceal his passion, and yet he longed perpetually for a chance to burst his fetters and fly to the rescue of his native land.

Before tracing his adventures further, let us return once more to Sweden. The dastardly escape of Christiern with the Swedish hostages had stung the whole country to the quick. Even the Chapter of Upsala, which had up to this time clung to the hope of restoring Trolle to his post, began to yield to the oft-repeated exhortations of the regent, and prepared to nominate a new archbishop. The man whom Sture urged for the position was the bishop of Strengnäs, one of those who had voted in favor of demolishing Stäket; and so early as the preceding February the chapter had practically assented to this choice. Nothing further, however, was done about it; and when, in the autumn of 1518, the papal legate with his proclamations of pardon appeared in Sweden, the chapter began to look toward him for help. Arcimboldo was not the man to let slip an opportunity to aggrandize himself. He therefore was prepared to listen impartially to the arguments on every side, and as papal legate to use his authority in favor of the highest bidder. Now, it required little sagacity to see that Trolle, whose cause the king of Denmark had commissioned him to urge, but who was at this time stripped of his prerogatives and in prison, could offer small reward; and from the king of Denmark he had already received quite as much as he had reason to expect. Moreover, it appeared from the experience of the last two years that Christiern's hopes of Sweden were likely to result in air. Sture was to all appearances the rising star, and on him the crafty legate resolved to fix his hopes. There seemed no valid reason, however, for deserting Christiern. It would be better so to trim his sails as to receive any emoluments that might be forthcoming from either party. He therefore approached the regent under the guise of mediator. The regent received him kindly, and covered him with honors and rewards. In the winter of 1518-1519 a meeting was held at Arboga at which the case of Trolle was laid before the legate. The outcome of it was that Trolle formally resigned his archbishopric and was restored to freedom. Shortly after, on the 5th of February, we find the legate reappointing the old archbishop, Ulfsson, to the post. Just why this course was taken it is impossible to state with certainty. But the reasons which led to it may easily be surmised. Ulfsson was a man of wealth, with few enemies and many friends. He was, next to Trolle, the choice of the Upsala Chapter and of Christiern, and he had already some time before been asked by Sture to reassume the post. To one of Arcimboldo's compromising temper it is not strange that Ulfsson should have seemed a person whose favor it was desirable to win.

Meantime the king of Denmark was not idle. He still clung to the strange infatuation that the people of Sweden might be persuaded to accept him as their king, and almost while in the act of seizing the Swedish hostages instructed Arcimboldo to beg the regent for a friendly conference. This wild proposal Sture treated with the contempt which it deserved. He wrote to Christiern a straightforward letter in which he refused to deal further with him, and demanded that the hostages be immediately returned. Christiern of course did not comply. On the contrary, he continued his warlike preparations, and throughout the whole of the next year, 1519, his fleet was busy in making incursions along the Swedish coast. These incursions, though they caused the regent great annoyance, had little permanent effect. The king was still smarting under his recent defeat, and did not venture at once to undertake another campaign on an extensive scale.

One thing the year 1519 did for Sweden. It ridded her of that consummate scoundrel Arcimboldo. After he had fleeced the regent and his people of every penny that they had to give, he set forth with his ill-gotten gains for Denmark. He soon learned, however, that he had been serving too many masters. Christiern had got wind of his ambassador's familiarity with the regent, and had sent out spies to seize him on his return. But the Italian proved more slippery than his royal master had supposed. Scarce had he set foot on shore when he perceived that Denmark was not the place for him. He embarked once more for Sweden, whence he soon crossed over to Germany on his way to more congenial climes. The last thing we hear of him is that the pope rewarded him with the Archbishopric of Milan.

FLIGHT OF GUSTAV; UPRISING OF THE DALESMEN. 1519-1521.

ONE morning, in the early autumn of 1519, a young man, clad in the coarse garments of a drover, made a hasty exit from the gate of Kalö Castle, and turning into the forest proceeded along the western shore of Kalö Bay. His step was firm and vigorous, and indicated by its rapidity that the wayfarer was endeavoring to elude pursuit. Though apparently not over twenty-four, there was something about the traveller's face and bearing that gave him the look of a person prematurely old. Of large frame, tall and broad-shouldered, with heavy massive face, high cheek-bones, a careworn dark blue eye, large straight nose, and compressed lips,—the under lip projecting slightly,—he would have been pointed out anywhere as a man not easily to be led. The face would not, perhaps, be regarded as particularly intellectual; but determination and energy were stamped on every feature, and every movement of the body displayed strength and power of endurance. It was pre-eminently the face and body of one made to govern rather than to obey. Such, in his twenty-fourth year, was Gustav Vasa. He had made his escape from Kalö Castle, and was fleeing with all speed to Lubeck, the busy, enterprising head of the Hanseatic League.

His way led him through some of the most picturesque spots in Denmark. It was a lovely rolling country, with fertile fields and meadows, relieved in places by little clumps of forest, beneath which he could often discern the time-worn front of some grim old mansion. Sheep and cattle were grazing on the hillsides. Thatch-roofed huts, with plastered walls, were all about him. The fields, in those September days, were red with buckwheat. Occasionally a broad meadow spread out before him, and, to avoid the husbandmen gathering in their crops, he was often forced to make a long circuit through thick forests of beech and maple. Here and there he came on mighty barrows raised over the bodies of Danish warriors and kings. Well might it make his blood boil within him to witness these honors heaped upon the Danes for their deeds of blood and cruelty to his fathers. Through such scenes, weary and footsore, in constant dread of his pursuers, and with dark misgivings as to the fate before him, he pressed on, until at last, near the end of September, the gray walls of Lubeck, to which he had looked forward as a refuge, stood before him and he entered in.

Lubeck, the capital of the Hanse Towns, and by virtue of this position monarch of the northern seas, had been for three centuries a bitter foe to Denmark. At intervals the Danish kings had sought to check the naval supremacy of Lubeck, and more than once the two powers had been at open war. Of late, by reason of dissensions among the Towns, Denmark had gradually been gaining the upper hand. But Lubeck was still very far from acknowledging the right of Denmark to carry on an independent trade, and the growing power of the Danish kings only added fuel to the flame. Lubeck was, therefore, at this time a peculiarly favorable asylum for one who was at enmity with Christiern. Gustav doubtless had reckoned on this advantage, and had resolved to throw himself on the mercy of the town. He went directly to the senate, laid his case before them, and asked them boldly for a ship and escort to take him back to Sweden. This request apparently was more than they were prepared to grant. They hesitated, and in the mean time the commandant of Kalö Castle tracked his prisoner to Lubeck, and appeared before the senate to demand that he be surrendered. Many of the senators, unwilling to incur the wrath of Christiern, were minded to give him up. Others, however, were opposed to such a course. As a result, all action in the matter was for the time suspended. Eight weary months dragged on, Gustav throughout that period remaining in Lubeck. Finally, in May, 1520, one of the burgomasters, whose friendship the youth had won, espoused his cause, and he was allowed to sail for Sweden. By good fortune he steered clear of the Danish fleet, and on the 31st of May set foot again on his native soil, near Kalmar.

Meantime the Danish arms had not been idle. Soon after the overthrow of Trolle and the destruction of his castle, the king of Denmark had despatched a messenger to Rome, to enlist the Holy Father in his cause. Pope Leo, reluctant to take upon himself to decide a matter of whose merits he could know so little, appointed the archbishop of Lund, aided by a Danish bishop, to investigate the question and report to him. A tribunal so composed could scarcely be expected to render other verdict than that which Christiern wished. They reported adversely to the regent. Sture and his adherents were therefore excommunicated by the pope, and all church ministrations interdicted throughout Sweden. To a pious people such a blow was terrible in the extreme. All church bells were for the moment hushed, the church doors barred, and the souls of an entire nation doomed to eternal death. But even in the face of this calamity the regent persevered. He refused to restore Trolle to his post, or even to make him amends for his losses. On this news being brought to Rome, the pontiff made no attempt to hide his wrath. He wrote at once to Christiern, with instructions to enter Sweden and inflict punishment on those who had thus set at naught the papal power. Christiern was entranced. As champion of the pope he felt certain of success. Without delay he collected all the forces in the kingdom, horse and foot, and placed them under the command of a gallant young officer, Otto Krumpen, with orders to invade Sweden from the south. They landed in the early days of January, 1520, and proceeded northwards, ravaging the country as they went. Sture at once issued a broadside to the people, calling them to arms. He likewise sent his messengers to Trolle, to beg him to use his influence against the enemies of Sweden. The deposed archbishop, now cringing before his victor, yielded his assent. Sture, thus emboldened, moved forward with his army to meet the Danes. Knowing that they were advancing through the province of Vestergötland, and that their line of march in the winter season would be across the lakes, Sture took up his position in a narrow cove at the northern end of Lake Åsunden. In the centre of this cove, through which the Danes must pass, he raised a huge bulwark of felled trees, and within the bulwark stationed his infantry, with provisions enough to last two months. He then chopped up the ice about the fort, and retired to the north with his cavalry to await the onset. It was not long he had to wait. On the 18th of January the Danish army drew near, and seeing the fortification began to storm it with their catapults. As they approached, the Swedish cavalry, with Sture at their head, dashed out along the shore to meet them. The regent was mounted on a fiery charger, and carried into the very thickest of the fight.

But scarcely had the first shot been fired when a missile glancing along the ice struck Sture's horse from under him, and in a moment horse and rider were sprawling on the ice. So soon as Sture could be extricated, he was found to have received an ugly wound upon the thigh. His followers bore him bleeding from the field, and hastened with his lacerated body to the north. But the battle was not yet over. Long and hot it raged about the fortress on the ice. Twice the Danish troops made a mad assault, and after heavy losses were repulsed. At last, however, their heavy catapults began to tell. The sides of the bulwark weakened, and the Danish army by a vigorous onslaught burst open a passage, and put the Swedish infantry to the sword. This victory was followed by a night of riot, the Swedes thus gaining time to collect the scattered remnants of their army. With a single impulse, though without a leader, they fled across the marshy meadows of Vestergötland to the north. Their goal was Tiveden, a dreary jungle of stunted pines and underbrush, through which it was expected the enemy would have to pass. Here after two days' march they gathered, and threw up a mighty barrier of felled trees and brushwood, thinking in that way to impede the passage of the Danes. All about them the land, though not mountainous, was rough and rugged in the extreme, huge bowlders and fragments of rock lying about on every side. In spots the undergrowth was wanting, but its place was generally filled by little lakes and bogs, quite as difficult to traverse as the forest. In this region the patriots collected, and with undaunted spirit once more awaited the coming of the Danes. Again they were not disappointed. The Danish army, recovering from its night of revelry, proceeded on the track of the fugitives, stormed their barrier, and on the 1st of February put them once more to flight. This done, the invaders pressed forward, burning, robbing, murdering, and affixing bans to every church door, till they arrived at Vesterås.

Let us turn for a moment to another scene. Sture, who had been carried bleeding from the field of battle, had been taken first to Örebro. But the journey over the ice and snow at the dead of winter so aggravated his wound that it was clear to all he could take no further part in carrying on the war. He gave orders therefore to be removed to Stockholm, where he might be under the tender care and sympathy of his wife. It was God's will, however, that he should never see her more. On the 2d of February, when almost within sight of the castle walls, he died; and the loved one for whose sympathy he had longed was given nothing but her husband's lifeless corpse. They buried of him all that earth could bury; but his undaunted spirit remained still among his people, cheering them in their misfortunes, and ever calling upon them to resist the hand of the oppressor. Sten Sture's character is one which draws forth a warmth of sentiment such as can be felt for no other character of his time. Living in an age when hypocrisy was looked upon with honor, and when falsehood was deemed a vice only when unsuccessful, he showed in all his dealings, whether with friends or foes, a steadfast integrity of purpose with an utter ignorance of the art of dissimulation. Not a stain can history fix upon his memory. Highly gifted as a statesman, courageous on the field of battle, ever courteous in diplomacy, and warm and sympathetic in the bosom of his family, his figure stands forth as one of the shining examples of the height to which human character can attain. It is with a sigh we leave him, and turn again to trace the history of his people.

Grim ruin now stared the patriot army in the face. Bereft of the only person who seemed competent to guide them, beaten at every point, without arms or provisions, and with a horde of trained and well-armed soldiers at their heels, the fleeing patriots came straggling into Strengnäs on the Mälar. Hubbub and confusion reigned supreme. Many of the magnates counselled immediate surrender. Others, somewhat more loyal to their country, raised a timid voice in favor of continuing the war, but no one ventured to come forth and lead his fellow-countrymen against the foe. Thus they frittered away the precious moments while the Danes were getting ready for another onset. All this time there was one brave heart still beating for them in the capital. The regent's widow, nothing daunted by her own calamity or by the disasters that had come upon her husband's people, kept sending messengers one after another to implore them to unite in defence of their native land. At length it seemed as if her supplications were destined to prevail. A firmer purpose spread among them, and they girded up their loins for another conflict. Their spark of courage, however, proved abortive. No sooner did the enemy again appear than the patriots turned their backs and fled in wild dismay. On coming once more together after this bloodless battle, they resolved without further ado to lay down arms. A letter was despatched to

Krumpen requesting parley. This was granted; and on the 22d of February it was agreed that the two parties should hold a conference in Upsala on the 3d of March, for the purpose of making terms. The Swedish party then urged Christina to attend the conference. She however turned a deaf ear to their entreaties, and sent off a despatch at once to Dantzic begging for aid against King Christiern; so the conference began without her. As a preliminary, Krumpen produced a document from the king of Denmark empowering him to offer terms of peace. This done, a proposition to declare allegiance to King Christiern was at once brought forward; and at the instance of Gustaf Trolle and the other Danish-minded magnates present, the proposal was finally accepted, though not until Krumpen had consented to certain terms on which the patriots insisted. These terms were that all past offences against the Danish crown should be forgiven, that all fiefs hitherto granted to their fellow-countrymen should be preserved, and that Sweden should continue to be governed in accordance with her ancient laws and customs. The document reciting these terms was issued on the 6th of March, and on the 31st it was confirmed by Christiern.

The main body of the Swedish nation being thus again in the hand of Denmark, it was expected that Christina would no longer dare to offer resistance. It was therefore resolved to approach her once more upon the subject. An armed body of some three thousand men was despatched forthwith to Stockholm, a couple of ambassadors being sent ahead to invite Christina to a conference outside the town. The reception which they met was such as to convince them that the regent's widow possessed, at any rate, a portion of her husband's courage. No sooner did they near the capital than the portcullis was raised and a volley fired upon them from within the walls. Thus discomfited, the ambassadors withdrew, and Krumpen, having insufficient forces to undertake a siege, returned to Upsala, and the Swedish forces that had joined him retired to their homes.

Christina was thus afforded a short respite in which to gather strength. The bravery and determination which she had displayed, even from the moment of her husband's death, already began to inspire confidence among the people. Most of the great men in the realm, intimidated by the threats or allured by the promises of Krumpen, had sworn allegiance to the king of Denmark. But the chief castles were still held by the patriots, and throughout the land there was a strong undercurrent of feeling against the Danes. In most parts the people were only waiting to see which way the wind was going to blow, and for the time being it seemed likely to blow in favor of the Swedes. The regent's widow used every effort to rouse the people from their lethargy, and with increased success. All winter long the king of Denmark was burning to send reinforcements, and dickering with the Powers of Europe to obtain the necessary funds. But his credit was bad, and it was only with great difficulty that he at last despatched a body of some fifteen hundred men. Christina, on the other hand, was being reinforced by the Hanse Towns along the Baltic, and in the early spring the current of sentiment had set so strongly in her favor that a plot was formed to drive off the Danish troops beleaguering the Castle of Vesterås, on the Mälar. So soon as this plot reached the ears of the Danish leader, he resolved to break the siege and hurry off to join the forces of Krumpen at Upsala. He did so; but he did so none too soon. He found his path beset by the peasantry lying in ambush in the woods, and before he succeeded in pushing through them, he was led into a bloody battle from which the patriots came off victorious, though their leader fell.

Emboldened by this success, Christina now sent a messenger among the peasantry to collect a force with which to attack the Danish army in Upsala. In a short space of time he had gathered a strong band of peasantry and miners, with whom, reinforced by a detachment from Stockholm, he marched forward to Upsala. As the patriots approached the town, a squad stationed by Krumpen outside the walls descried them and sounded the alarm. This was on Good Friday, April 6, 1520, and Krumpen was in the cathedral when the news arrived. Without delay he hurried forth and gave orders that every man, both horse and foot, should gird on his armor and assemble in the square. As soon as they had come together, he led them outside the town and drew up his line of battle close beneath the walls. In front of this line he formed a solid phalanx, with a wing on either side composed of horse and foot. Still farther ahead he placed his catapults, with the largest of which he opened fire first, the sharpshooters at the same time picking off the enemy. The sky was heavily overcast, and at the very beginning of the battle a driving storm with rain and sleet came beating down in the faces of the Danes, thus blinding them. Their cavalry, too, was almost useless; for the ground was covered with melting snow, which formed in great cakes under the horses' hoofs, and soon sent horses and riders sprawling on the ground. The patriots, however, being without cavalry or muskets, suffered little from the rain. They were not slow to take advantage of the opportunity thus afforded them, and pressed forward madly on the left wing until finally it began to yield. The standard-bearer, half frozen, was about to drop the standard, when a Danish veteran rushed forward, seized it from his hands, and fixed it in the nearest fence, at the same time shouting: "Forward, my men! Remember your own and your fathers' valor! Shall this standard of your country fall unstained into the hands of the enemy?" At these words the company rallied and, hacking at the hands of the patriots who strove to pluck the standard from the fence, compelled them to withdraw. This company then joined the others, and a long and bitter conflict followed, the two armies fighting face to face. At length, as soon as the snow began to be well packed, the Danish cavalry came to the front once more, and after a series of violent charges, broke in two places through the enemy's ranks. The patriots, now cut into three distinct bodies, fled in wild despair. One body of them was surrounded and massacred on the spot. Another fled to a brick-kiln near at hand, hoping thus to be sheltered from the fury of the Danes. But they were pursued, the whole place was set on fire, and all who issued from it were put to the sword. The third portion of the Swedes fled in terror to the river, but many of them weighted down by their arms were drowned. Thus ended a fearful battle. The snow was literally drenched with blood. Of the Swedes, who numbered 30,000, it is said two thirds were killed; while the Danes, 8,000 strong, lost half.

After this fearful slaughter both parties were for the nonce more cautious. Messengers were sent by each throughout the land to gain recruits, but they were careful to avoid a general conflict. Skirmishes and trickery were the order of the day. The patriots were frittering away their chances for lack of a leader, and Krumpen was waiting for the arrival of King Christiern. This was delayed only till the breaking of the ice. Towards the close of April, 1520, Christiern set sail with a large fleet for

Sweden, having on board the Archbishop of Lund and some other influential prelates, to lend to his expedition the aspect of a religious crusade. Proceeding first to Kalmar, he called upon the castle to surrender, but in vain. Seeing that his only mode of reducing the castle was by siege, he resolved for the present to give it up, and after issuing a broadside to the people of Vestergötland, summoning them to a conference to be held a month later, on the 3d of June, he advanced to Stockholm and dropped anchor just outside the town. This was on the 27th of May, four days before the landing of Gustav Vasa on the Swedish coast.

The arrival of Gustav Vasa marks an epoch in the history of Sweden. It is the starting-point of one of the most brilliant and successful revolutions that the world has ever known. Other political upheavals have worked quite as great results, and in less time. But rarely if ever has a radical change in a nation's development been so unmistakably the work of a single hand,—and that, too, the hand of a mere youth of four-and-twenty. The events immediately preceding the return of Gustav prove conclusively, if they prove anything, how impotent are mere numbers without a leader. For years the whole country had been almost continuously immersed in blood. One moment the peasantry were all in arms, burning to avenge their wrongs, and the next moment, just on the eve of victory, they scattered, each satisfied with promises that his wrongs would be redressed and willing to let other persons redress their own. What was needed above all else was a feeling of national unity and strength; and it was this feeling that from the very outset the young Gustav sought to instil in the minds of the Swedish people. As we now follow him in his romantic wanderings through dreary forest and over ice and snow and even down into the bowels of the earth, we shall observe that the one idea which more than any other filled his mind was the idea of a united Swedish nation. At first we shall find this idea laughed at as visionary, and its promoter driven to the far corners of the land. But before three years are over, we shall see a Swedish nation already rising from the dust, until at last it takes a high place in the firmament of European powers.

The memorable soil on which Gustav disembarked lay two miles south of Kalmar; and he hurried to the town without delay. Kalmar was at this time, next to Stockholm, the strongest town in Sweden. Lying on two or three small islands, it was guarded from the mainland by several narrow streams, while on the east it was made secure through a stupendous castle from attack by sea. This castle was at the time in charge of the widow of the last commandant, and was strongly garrisoned, as was also the town below, with mercenaries from abroad. On entering the town Gustav was received with kindness by the burghers, and sought in every way to rouse their drooping spirits. He even approached the German soldiers with a view to inspire comfort in their souls. But his words of courage fell on stony ground. It is the nature of mercenaries to fight like madmen when the prospect of reward is bright, but no sooner does a cloud gather on the horizon, than they throw down their arms and begin to clamor for their pay. Such at that moment was the state of things in Kalmar. Christiern, backed by the leading powers of Europe, and upheld in his expedition by the authority of Rome, had just arrived in Sweden with a powerful army, and was now lying at anchor in the harbor of the capital. The Swedish forces, broken in many places and without a leader, were gradually scattering to their homes. The cloud that had long been gathering over the head of Sweden seemed about to burst. The future was already black, and a listening ear could easily catch the mutterings of the approaching storm. The Kalmar mercenaries therefore were only irritated by the importunities of the youthful refugee, and it was only through the intercession of the burghers that he was saved from violence and allowed to leave the town.

To revisit the scenes of his boyhood and his father's house was no longer possible. The brave Sten Sture, from whose palace he had been stolen two years since, was lying beneath the sod; and Stockholm, held by the young man's aunt Christina, was in a state of siege. All access to her or to the capital would have been at the peril of his life. He therefore; renounced for the time being his desire to see his family, and proceeded stealthily to approach the capital by land. His way lay first across the dreary moors and swamps of Småland. Here he went from house to house, inciting the peasantry to rebel. Among others he sought out some of his father's tenants, in the hope that they at least would hear him. But he found them all sunk in lethargy, cowering under the sword of Christiern. His voice was truly the voice of one crying in the wilderness. The golden hope of lifting his country out of her misery seemed shattered at a blow. Instead of being received with open arms as a deliverer, he was jeered at in every town, and finally so bitter grew the public sentiment against him that he was forced to flee. Hardly daring to show his face lest he should be shot down by the soldiers of the king, he betook himself to a farm owned by his father on the south shore of the Mälar. Here he remained in secrecy through the summer, hoping for better times,—an unwilling witness of the subjugation of his land,—till finally he was driven from his refuge by an act of Christiern so revolting in its villany that it made the whole of Europe shudder.

Christiern, on the 27th of May, was riding at anchor in the harbor of the capital. Among his men was Hemming Gad, over the spirit of whose dream had come a vast change since his capture some eighteen months before. Just when this change began, or how it was effected, is unknown. But already, in March of 1520, the report had spread through Sweden that Gad had turned traitor to his native land, and we find him writing to the people of Stockholm to tell them that he and they had done Christiern wrong, and begging them to reconcile themselves to Christiern as he had done. Gad was a statesman,—a word synonymous in those days with charlatan,—and he did not hesitate to leave his falling comrades in order to join the opposite party on the road to power. Doubtless Christiern took care that he lost nothing by his change of colors, and doubtless it was with a view to aid himself that he brought Gad back to Sweden.

No sooner did Christiern arrive off Stockholm than Krumpen came with Archbishop Trolle from Upsala, to receive him. They held a council of war on board the fleet, and resolved to lay siege once more to Stockholm. The capital was by this time well supplied with food; but the summer had only just begun, and Christiern thought by using strict precautions to starve the town ere winter. Pitching his camp along the shore both north and south, and blockading the harbor on the east, he sent messengers through the land to enlist the peasantry in his cause. Many of them he propitiated by a generous distribution of salt which he had brought with him from Denmark. Things, however, were not entirely to his taste. Christina too had ambassadors inciting the people to revolt.

On the 27th of June a large body of the patriots laid siege to the palace of the bishop of Linköping. About the same time also the monastery of Mariefred, inhabited by the old archbishop Ulfsson, was threatened; and a throng of peasants marched to Strengnäs to burn and plunder. How crude the patriot forces at this time were is apparent from a letter from a Danish officer to Krumpen, in which it is said that out of a body of about three thousand only one hundred and fifty were skilled soldiers. Christiern finally deemed it best to send a force to Vesterås to storm the castle. This was done, the castle fell, and the officer in command was taken prisoner. It was now August, and the Stockholmers, no aid thus far having come to them from abroad, were losing heart. In this state of things the king sent Gad and others inside the walls to urge the people to surrender. Christina and her sturdy burghers received the messengers with scorn; but the magnates, already more than half inclined to yield, vehemently advocated the proposal. Soon the whole town was in an uproar. A riot followed, and some blood was shed. But at last Christina and her adherents yielded, and delegates were sent outside the town to parley. After several days of bickering it was agreed that Stockholm should be surrendered on the 7th of September next, but on the other hand that all hostility to Christiern and to his fathers, as well as to Archbishop Trolle and the other prelates, should be forgiven.

Two days later, on the 7th of September, the burgomasters crossed over in a body to Södermalm, and delivered the keys of the city gates into the hands of Christiern. Then, with bugles sounding and all the pomp and ceremony of a triumph, he marched at the head of his army through the city walls and up to the Great Church, where he offered thanksgiving to Almighty God. That over, he proceeded to the citadel and took possession. The same day and the day following he obtained two documents,—one from the Cabinet members then in Stockholm, and the other from the burgomaster and Council,—granting the castle to Christiern during his life, and at his death to his son Hans, or, if he should die before the king, then to the king's wife Elizabeth, to revert, after the death of all three, to the Cabinet of Sweden. Christiern then appointed his officers throughout the country, after which he sailed away for Denmark.

Not long, however, was Sweden freed from his contaminating presence. Within a month he had returned, breathing out threatenings and slaughter against the nation that he had vanquished. A general diet had been summoned to meet at Stockholm on the first day of November. As this diet was to be immediately followed by the coronation of the king, special efforts had been made to secure a large attendance of the Danish party. The venerable Ulfsson, now tottering to the grave, had recently written to Christiern that he would be present at the triumphal entry into Stockholm, "even if," as he says, "I have to crawl upon my knees;" and he was present at the diet. When the appointed day arrived, the delegates were summoned to a hill outside the town, and were shut in on every side by the pikes and rapiers of the royal soldiers. The proceedings were cut and dried throughout. A pompous oration was delivered by one of the king's satellites, declaring the grounds on which his master claimed the throne of Sweden, at the close of which the people were asked whether they would have him for their king, and with their tyrants' weapons brandished before their eyes they answered yes. With this elaborate farce the ceremony ended and the people scattered, being first ordered to return on the following Sunday and share in the coronation festivities of the king whom they had thus elected against their will. The ostentatious mummery of these mock ceremonies would cause a smile but for the frightful tragedy with which they were to close. None but the blindest partisans could have felt anything else than aversion for this monster on whose head they were to place the crown. Even his own friends hated him, and despised the very ground on which he trod. But it was the age of heaven-born rulers; so the masses bent their knee and sang their pæans to the demon whom fate had made their king.

It was on the 4th of November—a dreary Sunday—that the tragedy began. On that day, with a great flourish of trumpets and display of power, the monarch proceeded to the Great Church to be crowned. The huge edifice was filled to overflowing. From north and south, from mountain and valley, all of note in the three kingdoms had flocked thither on this day to behold the imposing spectacle. Gustaf Trolle, now once more archbishop, stood at the high altar, lined on either side by the six Swedish bishops and the Upsala Chapter. The whole chancel was one blaze of gold and silver; and as the king marched through the main aisle with his splendid retinue, every eye was bent upon him and every whisper hushed. Proceeding straight up to the high altar, he bent his knee before the God whose name he was now so soon to desecrate. Then the archbishop raised from the altar a crown of gold glittering with precious jewels, and placed it reverently upon the monarch's brow. The sacred rite of consecration over, the monarch rose and turning was met by a herald of Charles V., who came from his master bringing a fleece which he attached with chains of gold around the monarch's neck, thus receiving him into the great Burgundian League. After this, a throne was placed before the altar, and Christiern conferred the order of knighthood on Krumpen and some of his other officers. It was observed, however, that all thus honored were of Danish birth. With this the ceremony of consecration closed, and the whole concourse poured forth once more from the house of God.

During three days the whole town now was given over to mirth and merrymaking. These days seem like the lull that goes before a storm. All strife was ended, all past injuries forgotten. The future seemed full of promise, and the Swedish peasants went hurrying back to their firesides to tell their wives and children of the peace and blessings promised them by Christiern. But it was not yet. Scarce had the echo of warfare died upon the wind when a frightful tragedy took place in Stockholm which sent a thrill of horror to the heart of Europe. At noon on the Wednesday following the coronation all the Swedish magnates with the authorities of Stockholm were summoned to the citadel and ushered into the august presence of their king. As they ranged themselves about the great hall, the nobles and their wives, all wondering what this dismal summons meant, they heard the castle gates grate upon their hinges, and a cold shudder gradually spread among them, as the thought now flashed upon them for the first time that they were no longer free. They had been decoyed by the fulsome promises of their ruler into the trap which he had laid. The noose was already tightening around their necks. Before them, on the throne hallowed by memories of former rulers, sat their tyrant, grim and lowering. Not a trace of mercy was visible in his features. Through a long pause, awful in its uncertainty, they waited, the cold sweat fast gathering on their brows. At length the pause was ended. Archbishop Trolle, chuckling at the near prospect of his revenge, stepped forward and addressed the throne. He began by portraying in ardent language the sufferings he had undergone. He declared that the cathedral at Upsala had been plundered while he was being besieged in Stäket. He dwelt at great length on the wrong which had been done him in the destruction of his castle. He drew attention to the conspiracy entered into against him by certain of the magnates, and their united oath never again to recognize him as archbishop. Finally, he denounced the conspirators by name, and called upon the king to visit them with the punishment which they deserved. At this Christina was summoned before the throne and asked for an explanation of her husband's conduct. She was at first struck dumb with terror; then, recovering herself, she pleaded that her husband had been no more guilty than the other conspirators, as would appear from the document which they all had signed. Christiern, learning for the first time of this document, demanded that it be produced. When this was done, and the king had examined it to his heart's content, he gave it to his clerk to copy, and called on each of the signers in turn to answer for his act. Christiern with his Cabinet then withdrew, leaving the patriot leaders in the great hall guarded by a body of Danish soldiers. At dusk two Danish officers entered with lanterns, "like Judas Iscariot" says a contemporary, and the doomed magnates were led out to the tower and thrown into prison to await the morn. When day broke, Christiern ordered the trumpets sounded and proclamation made that no citizen should leave his house. About noon the condemned patriots were led from their dungeons to the Grand Square, and huddled together beneath the platform on which they were to bleed. The citizens had by this time been permitted to leave their houses and had gathered around the foot of the scaffold, from which they were addressed in soothing language by several of the Danish Cabinet, whose words however were interrupted by constant cries of the victims calling on their fellow-countrymen to avenge them. At last the agony of suspense was over. One after another the condemned mounted the scaffold and were decapitated with all the refinement of cruelty that the bloodthirsty monarch and his satellites could devise. Over seventy in all were slaughtered, and their gory bodies piled up in one promiscuous mass in the centre of the square. On the following day the scene of carnage was renewed, several suspected citizens being seized in their houses and dragged to the place of blood. One poor wretch was executed for no other reason than because he was discovered weeping at the sight of his friends' death. Not till the following Saturday was the carnage over and the weltering mass conveyed outside the town. The body of Sture, together with the body of one of his babes, was dug up by Christiern's orders and burned, and the property of all who were slaughtered was seized and confiscated. Having thus effected his diabolical purpose and ridded himself of the flower of the Swedish patriots, the gory monarch set his officers at the head of affairs, and taking Christina and her two boys with him, marched through the land to Denmark, where he threw Christina and her children into prison.

Through all that summer and autumn Gustav Vasa had been cooped up in his hiding-place on the Mälar. Once, in peril of his life, he had approached the venerable Archbishop Ulfsson and solicited his advice. But he found little comfort there. Ulfsson urged him to go boldly to Christiern and beg for mercy. He even offered to intercede for the young man, and encouraged him with the assertion that he had been included among those to whom the king had promised immunity at the surrender of Christina. Gustav, however, knew too well what reliance he could place on Christiern's word. With a downcast spirit he went back to his hiding-place, resolved to await further developments before he ventured forth. It was a time of harrowing suspense, the iron entering into his very soul. Each day brought new intelligence of the victories of Christiern and the gradual dismemberment of the Swedish forces. His hopes were already well-nigh shattered when the report was wafted across the lake that his father, along with the other patriot leaders, had been slaughtered in the capital. Horror-stricken and overwhelmed with grief, he sprang to his feet, resolved to brave death rather than prolong this agony. Buckling on his sword, he mounted one of his father's steeds, and set forth for the north, filled with the dream of rescuing his native land. It was near the 25th of November, and the scenery was well in keeping with the dreary thoughts that flooded the horseman's mind. The stern gnarled oaks along the wayside, twisting their leafless boughs athwart the sky, seemed as perverse as the Swedes whom he had vainly sought to rouse. Even the frosty soil beneath him, unyielding to his tread, recalled the apathy with which his fellow-countrymen had listened to his cries. Had he been fired solely by a love of Sweden, he would very likely long ere this have renounced his hopeless task. But a selfish purpose kept him in the path. He was a pariah, hunted down by his enemies, and driven through sheer necessity to play the patriot. It was liberty or death. And so he pushed on, resolved to mingle among the hardy mountaineers of Dalarne, and strive at all hazards to rouse the flagging pulses of their hearts.

Crossing Lake Mälar about four miles from his father's house, Gustav hurried through the forests north of the lake with all the speed that a patriot's zeal could lend. To one companioned by happier thoughts the journey in those late autumn days must have been filled with delight. Dalarne, through which his journey lay, is the paradise of Sweden. As its name imports, it is "the land of valleys." The whole province stands high above the sea, rising higher as we travel farther north. The hills which separate the valleys are mostly crowned with pine and fir, and down their sides run broad and gently sloping fields. Here and there the scenery is varied by a little hamlet nestling along the hillside. Little lakes, too, dot the surface of the land, and tiny brooks go babbling across the fields. One stream, famous in Swedish history, bisects the district from north to south, passing through various lakes, and finally pours its waters into the Baltic. This tortuous river, called the Dalelf, is in some places broad and majestic, while in others it is narrow and goes foaming like a cataract over the rocks. Along the banks of this stream Gustav traced his steps, making first for a village on Lake Runn, where an old Upsala schoolmate dwelt. Here he arrived some five days after he left his father's house, and presenting himself in peasant's dress was given refuge. However, he declared to no one who he was, probably wishing first to learn how his host and others were affected towards the king. While yet uncertain what course he should pursue, one of the servants noticed that he wore a gold-embroidered shirt, and told her master; and this, coupled with his language and general appearance, led to his discovery. He thereupon appealed to his old schoolfellow to shield him from his enemies, but in vain. The danger was too great; and though full of sympathy for the young refugee, he told him he must leave the place. Thus once more an outcast, Gustav hurriedly skirted the south shore of the lake, and after a narrow escape by breaking through the ice, reached the house of another schoolmate, who offered him protection and then went off to inform the Danish officers. From this catastrophe Gustav was rescued by a warning from his betrayer's wife, and had fled ere the officers appeared. His next asylum was some twenty miles farther north, where he found protection at the hands of the parish priest. The king's officers were now upon the scent. The whole province was alive to the fact that it was harboring within its borders the regent's ward. The strictest vigilance was therefore necessary in order to save his life. So the priest kept him but a week, and then hurried him some thirty miles farther through the woods to Rättvik, a hillside village at the eastern extremity of Lake Siljan. There he tarried several days, talking with the peasantry, and urging them to rebel against the tyranny of their Danish ruler. He was now on ground to be ever afterwards famous in Swedish history. Here for the first time his words were heard with some degree of favor. The proud spirits of these mountain peasants had been already often roused by evidences of foreign usurpation, and it needed little to induce them to rebel. But their isolated position in a measure saved them from the burdens of the Danish yoke, and they answered they could venture nothing till they had held a conference with their neighbors. The disheartened outlaw therefore set forth once more. He traversed the icy meadows that lie along the eastern side of Lake Siljan, and after a journey of about twenty-five miles reached the village of Mora, lying at the head of the lake. It was on Christmas day that he addressed the people of this village. Knowing this to be his last hope of success, he took his stand on an elevated mound, and gazed over the white fields, dotted here and there with little hamlets, and to the snow-clad hills beyond. The surroundings added even to the zeal with which his own needs made him speak. He portrayed in burning terms the wrongs and insults that had been heaped upon the Swedish people. He alluded to his own affliction and to the general scene of carnage that had taken place in Stockholm. He pictured the evils in store for the proud highlanders before him, and appealed to them in the name of Almighty God to join him in a war for liberty. But all this eloquence was wasted. His appeal struck no responsive chord. The people flatly refused to give him their assistance. He had, therefore, but one course left. With no further hope of keeping his whereabouts unknown, he hastened with all speed from the town, and fled over the ice-bound hills of the west, to seek a last asylum in the wilds of Norway.

Black indeed were the clouds now gathering over the head of

Sweden. Even the liberty-loving province of Dalarne had refused to strike a blow for freedom. Soon, it seemed, the whole of Sweden would be groaning under the burden of a foreign despotism. Yet such an issue was by the design of Providence to be averted. But a few days after the flight of Gustav out of Mora news arrived that Christiern was preparing a journey through the land, and had ordered a gallows to be raised in every province. Rumor was rife, too, with new taxes soon to be imposed. Nor was it long before a messenger arrived who confirmed the words of Gustav as to the cruelties in Stockholm, and added further that there were many magnates throughout the realm who not only had not bowed the knee to Christiern, but had declared that rather than do so they would die with sword in hand. Then the blood of the villagers of Mora boiled within them. Post-haste, and trembling lest it were now too late, they put men on the track of the young fugitive with orders to push on by day and night and not rest till they had found Gustav and brought him back. They found him on the very frontier of Norway, and announced to him that their people were ready to join his banner and with him pour out their blood for freedom. With a joyous heart he turned about and hurried back to Mora. The whole province was now awake. Rättvik had already had a conflict with a body of Danish horsemen; and when the outcast hero appeared once more at Mora, he found a vast throng of peasants flocking from every side to join his ranks. By common consent he was chosen to be their leader and a body of sixteen stout highlanders selected to be his guard. This was in the early days of 1521. The perseverance of the stanch young outlaw was rewarded, and the supremacy of Gustav Vasa had begun.

WAR OF INDEPENDENCE; ELECTION OF GUSTAV TO THE THRONE. 1521-1523.

THERE are periods in the history of most nations when all that has been hallowed by time and custom seems of a sudden to lose its sanctity and bow down before the commanding influence of some new force. These periods are of rare occurrence and generally of short duration. They remind one of those thunderstorms which burst upon us at the close of a sultry August day, unheralded but by the stifling heat of a burning sky, and in a few moments leaving the atmosphere behind them pure and clear and cool. Sudden and unheralded as they appear, they are yet the direct result of a long series of forces, whose ultimate issue might have been accurately predicted did we but thoroughly understand the forces themselves. So, too, it is with great political upheavals. The revolution which drenched the whole of France with blood in 1789 is no more difficult to explain than the thunderstorm which drenches the parched earth with rain on a hot midsummer night. It was simply the reaction after a century of oppression, extravagance and vice. In like manner the great revolution whose development we are about to trace was merely the natural result of long years of tyranny culminating in the fearful carnage of the autumn of 1520. The Revolution in Sweden is, however, in one respect pre-eminent among the great crises known to history. Never was a revolution so thoroughly the work of a single man as that in Sweden. From beginning to end there was one figure whose presence alone infused life into a lukewarm people, and who, working upon the forces which had been forged by years of tyranny, shaped them gradually to his own commanding will. The Revolution in Sweden is the history of Gustav Vasa. He it was who set the torch, and he, too, pointed out the direction in which the flame should burn.

Early in January, 1521, the war of independence already had begun. By this time news of the revolt in Dalarne had spread throughout the land, and the Danish officers were wild with irritation that the young Gustav had escaped their clutches. The charge of affairs, at the withdrawal of Christiern, had been placed in the hands of a wretch scarce less contemptible than his master. This was one Didrik Slagheck, a Westphalian surgeon who, we are told, had "ingratiated himself with Christiern and ravished the wives and daughters of the Swedish magnates." Gad, for a time the councillor of the Danish king, was now no more. Christiern, shrewdly divining that one who had deserted his former master might desert again, had used him to mediate for the surrender of Stockholm and had then removed his head. In place of the old burgomaster and Council of Stockholm, the city was now held by satellites of Christiern, and any whose hearts revolted against his sickening cruelties were discreet enough to hold their tongues. Dalarne had become the only spot in Sweden where liberty still lived, and thither all liberty-loving Swedes whose hands were not yet tied repaired. Whenever these recruits appeared, Gustav placed them in the midst of his little army, and called upon them to declare what they had seen of Christiern's deeds. It makes a striking picture, this little band of patriots, in a far-off mountain region in the dead of winter, with no arms but their picks and axes, strong only in their high resolve, and yet breathing defiance against the whole army of the Danish king. Gustav knew the Swedish people well. He knew them slow to move, dull of intellect, and averse from reason. But he knew also that they were ardent in their emotions, permeated with a love of liberty, courageous in defence of their ancestral rights; and he foresaw that if he could once but rouse their passions by a vivid picture of Danish tyranny, he could make of them the finest soldiers in all Christendom. By Lent the little army was four hundred strong. With this force Gustav marched to the great copper-mine at Falun, where he seized the Danish steward and took possession of the royal rents, as well as of a quantity of clothing and some silk which he at once turned to a good use as banners for his army. He then retired to his camp, but shortly after returned, this time fifteen hundred strong. This rapid increase in his forces produced an instantaneous effect. No sooner did he appear than the miners joined his ranks, and further than that they wrote to their friends in all the neighboring provinces to join him too. Gustav then fixed the headquarters of his army near the southern boundary of Dalarne, and started, April 3, on a journey in person through several of the northern provinces to enlist recruits.

Meantime Slagheck had concentrated the Danish forces in and near the Castle of Vesterås, deeming this the best point at which to hold the patriots at bay. One detachment, indeed, proceeded north as far as the Dalelf, on the southern frontier of Dalarne, and encamped there, thinking to prevent the enemy from crossing. While waiting, the Danish leader is said to have inquired the population of Dalarne, and on being told that it was about twenty thousand, to have asked how the province could support so many. The answer was that the people were not used to dainties, that their only drink was water, and in hard times their only food a bread made from the bark of trees. "Even the Devil," ejaculated the officer, "could not vanquish men who live on wood and water;" and with that he ordered a retreat. Before they got off, however, the Swedes fell upon them and drove them home in flight. About the same time the burgomaster and Council of Stockholm despatched a letter to the northern provinces, urging them to pay no heed to the lies of Gustav; and Archbishop Trolle, after several epistles of a like nature, set sail along the coast of the Baltic to the north to use his influence in quelling the insurrection. But wherever he tried to land he was met by the peasantry with threats and imprecations; and he soon beat a hasty and ignominious retreat.

On returning from his recruiting-tour to the headquarters of his army, Gustav put his men through a regular course of training. Most of them were farmers, with scarce enough knowledge of military affairs to distinguish a javelin from a flagstaff. Their weapons were of the rudest sort,—axes and bows and arrows. He therefore taught them first of all to forge javelin and arrow heads. He also introduced a pike with spiral point which could be driven into a man's armor so as to hold him fast. To meet the necessities of a soldier, who was prevented by his occupation from paying for his goods with wheat or rye, Gustav issued a copper coin which was at once received as money. These preparations seem all to have been made with the prospect of a long-continued war. While they were in progress, a letter came from the burgomaster and Council of Stockholm, dated April 10, and addressed to the people of Dalarne, informing them that a number of vessels had just arrived from the Hanse

Towns, laden by order of Christiern with clothing and food, which were to be distributed among the people. After administering this mealy morsel the letter of the burgomaster and Council went on to urge the Dalesmen to have nothing to do with the lies and treachery of Gustav, but to consider their own and their children's welfare and bow humbly before their gracious king. This letter seems not to have produced the effect that was intended. Another that came about the same time was more effective. It was from some German soldiers who declared, with more or less exaggeration, that they were four thousand strong, that they had come to lend their succor to Gustav, had already seized nine of Christiern's best men-of-war, and expected within a few days to get possession of Stockholm. The news of this marvellous achievement seems never to have been confirmed, but at all events it fanned the enthusiasm of the infant army.

Discontent had by this time spread throughout the land. On the 18th of April we find the Danish authorities in Stockholm writing that tumult and confusion reign in all parts of the kingdom, and on the 23d of April they write of an insurrection that has broken out in Stegeholm. This rapid spread of the conflagration made it necessary for the Danish officers to increase their vigilance, and on the 26th of April they found an opportunity to win their spurs. It occurred in this wise. One of the recruiting-officers of Gustav, in his eagerness to advance the patriot cause, had pushed south into the very heart of the enemy's country, and finally burst into the town of Köping. Here, with all the rashness of a new-made officer, he let loose his soldiers on the town. The result was just what might have been expected. Ere nightfall the whole army, officers and men, were drunk. They retired to their camp, built blazing fires, and lay down to sleep without watch or guard. News of the situation was carried at once to Vesterås, where a force of three thousand men was got together and sent post-haste to Köping. It reached the patriot camp soon after midnight on April 26. The scene of debauchery was not yet past. The Danes fell upon them as they lay there in their drunken stupor, and slew them.

Three days before this catastrophe Gustav divided his entire forces into two parts, placing one under the command of an officer named

Olsson and the other under one Eriksson. He then reviewed his troops, and prepared to march against the Castle of Vesterås. He had planned an attack on the east side of the castle, and the force sent down to Köping had been given orders to attack it simultaneously on the west. On learning of the disaster at Köping he seems to have made no change in his own manoeuvres. He waited till the 29th, and then advanced to the walls of Vesterås. His design was not to attack the town that day. But the Danish soldiers, chafing for the fight and already glorying in success, gave him no choice. They came boldly forth to meet him, led by a line of cavalry, who dashed upon the patriots, so runs the chronicle, "like raging lions." The patriots received the charge like men. In their front rank were the halberdiers, armed with sharp weapons some fifteen or twenty feet in length. With these they kept the cavalry at bay, and worried the horses till at length confusion began to spread along the line. No sooner did the patriots see this than they discharged a volley of arrows, hitherto reserved. Under this double discomfiture, from their own horses and their opponents' arrows, the cavalry yielded, then finally turned and fled, leaving four hundred dead upon the field. Nor was this all. As the cavalry, frenzied with terror, dashed through the town-gate, they found the narrow streets blocked with the infantry, on whom their ungovernable steeds rushed with all the fury lent by fear. A large number were thus trampled to death, while the rest were precipitated into flight. Eriksson followed them a short distance, and then retired; but meantime Olsson entered the city from another quarter, and got possession of the enemy's cannon, ball, and powder. This he carried to Gustav, who had taken up his position on a ridge to the north of the town. When now the garrison saw that they were worsted, they set fire to the town and then retired to the castle. At this many patriots rushed back into the burning town, burst open the shops and wine-vaults, and parted their booty among them. As soon as the Danes saw what was going on, their courage once more rose, and they fell upon the plundering patriots, already half drunk with wine. Gustav therefore sent a detachment under Olsson into the town to drive the Danish soldiers back. They met in the public square, and a long and bloody battle followed; but at last the remnant of the Danish soldiers fled and took refuge in the monastery. Here they remained three weeks, and then escaped by boat to Stockholm. Gustav, after the fight was over, entered the town and destroyed every wine-cask in the place. Though the town had fallen, the Castle of Vesterås still held out. Experience, however, had made clear that it could not be reduced except by siege. He therefore pitched his camp on the west side of the castle, and despatched the main body of his forces to other parts.

First of all, he ordered Eriksson and Olsson to attack Upsala. They therefore proceeded with a body of infantry to a forest some twelve miles from the city, and pitched their camp. As soon as the canons, with the burgomaster and Council, heard that the city was to be attacked, they sent a letter to the patriots urging them to postpone the onset till after the 18th of May, Saint Erik's day, that they might celebrate the festival. But their messenger brought back answer that as Saint Erik's day was a Swedish festival, the patriots would enter the town before that day and attend to the festival themselves. However, the archbishop's steward, who held command of the town, felt no anxiety; and out of bravado gave a sumptuous feast one evening on the esplanade. The festivities were protracted with song and dance till after midnight; and scarce had the sound of revelry died away, when the patriots, warned of the midnight orgies, burst upon the town, beat down the guard, and held possession of the streets before any of the carousers knew they were at hand. So soon as they did come to their senses they poured a volley from their arquebuses into the spot where they thought the enemy were collected. But they were aiming in the dark, and not a finger of the Swedes was hurt. The archbishop's steward then planned a strategic movement on the rear, and endeavored to move his troops through a long wooden passageway running from the palace to the cathedral; but the Swedes, perceiving it, set fire to the passageway, and at the same time shot blazing arrows up into the palace roof. The Danes retaliated by setting fire to the buildings all about the palace; but the patriots in each case extinguished the fire before it got fully under way. The palace, however, was soon a mass of flames; and the archbishop's forces, seeing all was lost, mounted their steeds, burst open the palace-gate, and galloped in all haste over the fields to the south. The Swedes pursued, but, finding the enemy's steeds too fleet for them, showered a volley of arrows after the flying horsemen, and returned.

Early in June Gustav came from Vesterås, and opened negotiations with the canons of Upsala, with a view to win them over to his side. As they refused, however, to take action without consulting the archbishop, he begged them to consult him at once, and he himself wrote a pacific letter urging the archbishop to champion his country's cause. Trolle, then in Stockholm, scorned the message and seized the messenger who brought it. Then he placed himself at the head of a troop of three thousand foot and five hundred horse, in glittering armor, and marched to Upsala, declaring that his answer to the message he would convey in person. Gustav, expecting daily the return of his messenger, was taken wholly unawares. The great body of his soldiers had gone back to their farms, and he had but six hundred of them left. With these it would be madness to withstand the archbishop's force. He therefore evacuated the city, and hurried over the meadows to the west. As soon as he was out of danger, he despatched officers to call back the farmers to his ranks, and meantime drew up an ambuscade on the road between Stockholm and Upsala, thinking to spring upon the archbishop as he returned. The plot was discovered, and when the troops returned they took another path. Gustav, however, did not give up the chase. With his ranks once more replenished, he pursued the enemy, and a battle followed so hot that when the archbishop arrived at Stockholm, he entered the town with only an eighth part of the glittering troop with which he had started out.

The patriot army now proceeded to the capital, and pitched their camp on the hill north of the town. There they found four gallows from which were hanging the bodies of four Swedes, murdered to glut the rapacity of their Danish masters. One day, while encamped on this spot, the Danes came out against them, and dividing their forces into two bodies stormed the Swedish redoubt simultaneously on both sides. The charge was fierce, and lasted half a day, when the Swedes were driven from their stronghold with heavy loss, and forced to take up a new position about twelve miles farther north. There they remained three weeks, battling daily with the enemy with varying success. At last the commandant of Stockholm had recourse to strategy. Advancing with a powerful army till near the vicinity of the Swedish camp, he halted and placed his force in ambuscade. He then pushed forward with some forty horse and a few weak infantry to the enemy's earthworks, as if to storm them. After a slight skirmish, in which some eight or ten of the horse were captured, the Danish leader shouted that all was lost, and took to flight. The patriots, all unsuspecting, dashed after them, and followed blindly into the very midst of the Danish army, into the jaws of death. Thus ended the first attempt of Gustav Vasa to capture Stockholm.

Better fared it with him in other parts. One of the most valiant officers of Gustav was Arvid Vestgöte. This man was despatched, about the middle of May, to the provinces south of Stockholm, to enlist the peasantry in the Swedish cause. Collecting his forces along the way, he advanced from one town to another, plundering the estates of all who would not join him, and before the end of June reached Stegeborg, a strongly fortified castle on the Baltic coast. This he proceeded to besiege. In July, Norby, the most famous naval officer of Christiern, came to the rescue of the beleaguered castle with sixteen men-of-war. Landing his forces on the shore, he drew them up in battle-array, three hundred strong. The Swedes, however, rushed furiously upon them, and drove them to the sea. A few days later, after provisioning the castle, Norby sailed away to Denmark.

All through this spring and summer Gustav was busy passing from camp to camp, giving orders as to the disposition of his forces, and receiving the allegiance of the people. His practice, as far as possible, seems to have been to use persuasion, and only when that failed did he resort to force. This method proved successful in a marvellous degree. One after another the provinces recognized him as their leader; and on the 14th of July we find him issuing a proclamation as commander of five provinces, named in the order of their declaration of allegiance. His greatest difficulty at this time was in finding the means with which to pay his men. Possessing no authority to levy taxes, he was often forced to close the mouths of his clamoring soldiers by allowing them to plunder. The great body of his army was of course made up of Swedes. These were fighting for the welfare of their wives and children, and were content if he provided them only with the necessities of life. The mercenaries whom he employed were few. One of them, a tough old warrior named Rensel, has left us a chronicle of his life. He tells us he came over from Livonia in the winter of 1521, and was among the four thousand German veterans that counted on entering Stockholm in the spring. Gustav sent him back to the Continent for more men and ammunition; and when he returned in July of that year, he brought back sixty mercenaries with him. In August Gustav made an inspection of the camp at Stegeborg. While there, he learned that the Bishop of Linköping was more than half minded to join the patriot cause. This bishop, Hans Brask, was a man of rare shrewdness, excellent common-sense, and as time-serving as any man in Europe. He had strong convictions, but he always looked to see how the wind was blowing before he spoke them out. He had, among others, signed the decree for the demolition of Stäket, but had taken the precaution to place under his seal a slip of paper declaring that he affixed his signature perforce, and when his fellows were brought out to be beheaded, he removed the seal; by this little bit of Romanism he saved his head and the emoluments of his priestly office. To this man Gustav wrote in August, asking for a conference. The aspect of the heavens was not such as to justify the wily bishop in refusing. The continued brutality of Didrik Slagheck had raised such a storm of indignation in the country, that his own followers had found it necessary, on June 16, to hurry him out of Sweden, and announce that they had thrown him into jail. Nearly all of Sweden, except the fortified castles, was in the patriots' hands. The forces of Gustav were growing stronger day by day, and in the continued absence of Christiern the fortresses that still held out were likely soon to yield for want of food and ammunition. In this state of affairs Hans Brask made up his mind without delay. He granted the interview with Gustav, and was very easily persuaded to join the Swedish cause. It now seemed best that the vague authority conferred upon Gustav by the different provinces should be defined, so that he might as representative of the Swedish nation treat with foreign powers. He therefore announced that a general diet would be held at Vadstena on August 24, and all the chief men of different classes in the kingdom were summoned to attend. By whom the delegates were selected we are not told. Certainly they were not selected by Gustav. At all events, they came together in vast numbers, and, if we are to believe the chronicle, urged Gustav to accept the crown. This, however, he refused, but accepted the title of Commander of the Swedish Army, at the same time adding that after they had wholly freed themselves from Christiern, a general diet might then be held to discuss the propriety of choosing some man of their own nation king.

While the patriots were occupied with their diet, the Danes in Stockholm sent a force by water to the relief of Vesterås. The patriots, still in possession of the town, sought by aid of their falconets to prevent a landing, but without avail. The relief-party made its way into the castle, replenished it with men and ammunition, and withdrew. Gustav, knowing that the Danes on their return to Stockholm must pass through a narrow inlet some thirty yards in width, sent thither a force to throw up earthworks on both sides of the passage and await the coming of the enemy. The battle which ensued was fierce, and lasted two whole days; but finally, having inflicted as well as suffered heavy loss, the Danish fleet escaped. Shortly after, in September, Gustav sent a force to Finland. This force received large reinforcements from the people in that province, and on the 24th of November, being furnished ammunition by the bishop of Åbo, laid siege to Åbo Castle. On December 18 the Castle of Stegeborg still besieged by Arvid Vestgöte, fell; and the commandant, Berent von Mehlen, after two months in prison swore fealty to Gustav. Six days after the castle yielded, Norby, not having heard of the disaster, came sailing boldly into the harbor with food and men. The patriots soon informed him of his error by firing upon him from the castle walls, and in the conflict which took place it is reported that six hundred of his men were lost. Most of Vestgöte's forces, after the fall of Stegeborg, were transferred to the vicinity of Stockholm, to which Gustav early in the autumn had again laid siege. The summer's experience had made manifest that it would be useless to assault the capital. Gustav therefore held his forces several miles away from the city, and with a view to cut off supplies divided them into three camps,—one on the north, another on the south, and the third on an island to the west. On Christmas eve the garrison, finding that no assault was likely to be made, embarked some fifteen hundred men on yawls and coasting-vessels, and proceeded against the island-camp. The Swedish leader watched the preparations from a hill; and when he saw that the enemy were coming against himself, divided his men into squads of fourteen and sixteen, and placed these squads at intervals through the woods with orders to sound their horns as soon as the neighboring squad had sounded theirs. He then waited till the enemy were all on shore, when he gave the signal, and in a moment it was re-echoed all along the line. The effect was marvellous. The enemy, horrified by the apparent number of the Swedes, turned and fled. The Swedes, who had but about four hundred and fifty men in all, pursued them to their boats and cut down two hundred of them on the shore. After this the garrison from time to time made raids upon the northern and southern camps, and generally got the better of the Swedes, though nothing of marked importance was accomplished by either side. On the 30th of January the Castle of Vesterås, hard pressed for food and cut off from supplies, surrendered. Later in the winter, seemingly in March, Norby came from Denmark with a large force to Stockholm, and replenished the garrison with fresh men. About the same time the Swedish camp on the north was moved nearer; and the Danes, thus reinforced by Norby, came out against them April 17, and routed them with heavy loss. The day following, a like sally was made on the southern camp with like result. Having thus raised the siege of Stockholm, Norby set sail for Finland, and routed the Swedish forces still besieging Åbo. The bishop of Åbo, finding his own land too hot for him, embarked for Sweden; but his vessel foundered, and all on board were drowned. In April Gustav recruited a strong force in Dalarne and the other northern provinces, and pitched his camps once more to the north and south of Stockholm.

The war had now been raging over a year, and Gustav had experienced the utmost difficulty in obtaining money with which to pay his men. In the absence of any authority to levy taxes, he had resorted to the practice of coining money, and had established mints in several places through the realm. His coins, which were known as "klippings," consisted of copper with a very slight admixture of silver, and twenty-four of them were issued for a mark. As a matter of fact their actual value fell far below what they purported to be worth. For such a practice it is difficult to find excuse, except that it was a practice universal at the time. Why a monarch should be justified any more than an individual in giving a penny where he owed a pound, is difficult to comprehend. Yet this had been for centuries the custom, and each successive monarch had pared a little from the standard, so that in the eight hundred years preceding Gustav Vasa the various monetary units all over Europe had declined to little more than an eighteenth part of their original value. In Denmark the debasement of the currency had been more rapid than in almost any other land, and the "klippings" of Christiern II. fell farther below their nominal value than any coin in Europe—till the "klippings" were issued by Gustav, which were a trifle worse than those of Christiern. Of course, as the standard of currency is lowered, its buying-power gradually declines, so that ultimately, under whatever name a particular coin may go, it will buy no more than could be had for the actual bullion which it contains. A mark in the sixteenth century would have bought, provided the relative supply of bullion and merchandise remained the same, only an eighteenth part of what it bought originally. The aim of monarchs was, therefore, to get rid of their debased coins at more than the real value, and after they had depreciated, to get them back at the depreciated value, melt them down, and lower the standard further. Precisely how much Gustav made by tampering with the currency is impossible to say, for there is no means of determining how many of his "klippings" he threw upon the market. It is clear, however, that the scheme was from a financial point of view successful, and that a vast number of the "klippings" were absorbed before the public detected their inferiority.

Unquestionably the marvellous progress made by Gustav in this first year of the revolution was owing in great measure to the critical state of things in Denmark. Christiern had by this time made enemies all over Europe. Lubeck, always a latent enemy, was particularly imbittered by Christiern's favoritism of the market towns of the Netherlands and his avowed intention of making Copenhagen the staple market for his kingdom; France hated him because he was the brother-in-law of her enemy, Charles V.; Fredrik, Duke of Schleswig-Holstein, opposed him because he had laid claim to those dominions; and his own clergy opposed him because of his rumored leaning towards Lutheranism and his efforts to check their power. All these things prevented his return to Sweden, and conspired against his credit so that he was unable to raise an army of any strength. Didrik Slagheck, too, whom he had placed at the head of affairs in Sweden, had fallen into disgrace, and, to appease the public clamor, had been beheaded. Even Gustav Trolle, after several attempts to exert his papal authority in Sweden, had found the land too hot for him, and for the present had withdrawn to Denmark.

Norby was at this time the most valuable officer that Christiern had. He infested the shores of the Baltic with his fleet, making frequent incursions on the land to plunder; and at length became so obnoxious that Gustav sent to Lubeck for a fleet. On the 7th of June it came, ten ships of war, laden with all sorts of merchandise, and fully equipped with powder, shot, and men. For this aid Gustav is said to have paid an enormous figure, giving his promissory note for the amount. Picking out a battalion of five hundred men, he sent them down to Kalmar, to which castle Vestgöte had just laid siege. The rest of the reinforcements he despatched to Stockholm, quartering them in his different camps, and then discharged all of the Swedish peasants except the young unmarried men. Shortly after this change the commandant of Åbo Castle crossed the Baltic with a powerful fleet, and sought to break the siege of Stockholm. But the Swedish fleet met him outside the harbor, captured or burnt his vessels, and took him prisoner. In October, seeing that the garrison was losing strength, Gustav advanced his camps nearer to the town. His southern camp he moved to Södermalm, from which he built a pontoon bridge to connect it with the west camp now on an island some three or four hundred yards from Stockholm. Another bridge he threw across the channel east of the city, and built upon it a turret which he armed with heavy guns. The city was thus hemmed in on every side, and a contemporary writes, "We cannot find in any of the old chronicles that Stockholm ever was so hard besieged before." Unless relief came it was merely a question of time when the garrison would have to yield. Once, in November, Norby came sailing into the harbor with five ships-of-war; but the Swedish fleet, consisting of fifteen vessels, drove him off, and, were it not for the half-heartedness of the German mercenaries, would very likely have destroyed his fleet.

The high spirit of the garrison had fallen. Wasted in numbers, with hunger and dissension spreading fast among them, and with scarce enough ammunition to resist an assault upon their walls, they waited impatiently for the army of Christiern, and marvelled that it did not come. All servants, old men, monks, burghers, and prostitutes they sent away, that there might be fewer mouths to feed. Each day, too, their numbers were diminished through the desertion of able-bodied men who escaped through the gates or over the walls and made their way by one means or another to the Swedish camp. There being no longer possibility of driving off the enemy by force, they felt that their only hope was fraud. They therefore one day sent a Swedish magnate to the enemy, with instructions to pretend that he had fled, and after finding out how matters stood, set fire to the camp and either return to the garrison, or, that being impossible, make his way to Denmark and induce the monarch to send immediate relief. This piece of stratagem, however, proved abortive; for two refugees from the garrison came forward and denounced the magnate as a spy.

When winter came, Gustav sent a large part of his army, chiefly the cavalry, to take up winter-quarters in Upsala. Others were sent to other towns. Some, too, were sent, in February, 1523, to the Norwegian frontier to gain the allegiance of the people. Towards the close of winter Gustav ordered his German troops to the south of Sweden on a similar errand, but within six weeks they came back and reported that the spring freshets had carried away the bridges and they could not proceed. Norby meantime lay with a strong force in the town and castle of Kalmar, and was making preparations to attack Vestgöte, who was still carrying on the siege, as soon as spring should open. But just as he was getting ready, he received word from the Danish Cabinet that Christiern had been deposed in Denmark, and Fredrik, duke of Schleswig-Holstein, summoned to the throne. At this news he set sail with all his force for Denmark, leaving only sixty men to hold the castle and town of Kalmar. Their orders were to form two garrisons of thirty each, one to guard the castle and the other to guard the town; and if through assault or failure of provisions they could not maintain the stronghold, they were to slaughter all the Swedes in Kalmar, set fire to the town, and sail to Gotland. As soon as the burghers of Kalmar learned of these instructions, they sent a messenger to the Swedish camp to tell the Swedes to enter the town by the north gate on the 27th of May, when the burghers would take care that the gate should be opened for them. On the day appointed Vestgöte advanced with all his cavalry, and drew them up in battle-array along the west and south side of the town as if to storm the southern gate. The garrison, all unsuspecting, flocked to that point in order to receive the charge. But meantime the Swedish infantry had massed themselves outside the northern gate, which at a concerted signal was thrown open on its hinges, and the infantry pressed in. It was but the work of a moment to put the little garrison to the sword. For a few weeks more the castle refused to yield, and it was not till the 7th of July that, reduced to the last extremity, it fell.

Kalmar had not yet fallen when it became clear that the war of independence was drawing to its close, and it was felt on every hand that the country had been too long without a king. The powers which Gustav possessed as regent were too vague to meet the necessities of a time of peace. While the army was in the field, he had authority, as commander of the forces, to levy the taxes necessary to sustain his men; but, so soon as the war was over, there would be no means for raising the money needed to pay the nation's debts. He therefore, shortly before the fall of Kalmar, summoned a general diet to be held at Strengnäs on the 27th of May. Whether or not all the magnates of Sweden were summoned to the diet is not known, but at any rate the peasantry were represented. The wily Brask, who had once saved his head by a bit of strategy, dared not put it in jeopardy again, and fearing that matters of weight might be brought before the diet, was suddenly taken ill and rendered unable to attend. The Cabinet, hitherto the sum and substance of a general diet, was practically dead, having been carried off in the fearful slaughter of 1520. One of the first things to be done, therefore, after the opening of the diet, was to fill these vacant seats. This was accomplished on the 2d of June, but whether the members were chosen by Gustav or by vote of the general diet we are not told. Noteworthy it is, that the persons selected, nine in number, were all of them laymen and warriors in the service of Gustav. Four days later, on the 6th of June, the question of electing a king of Sweden was brought before the house. The proposal was received with shouts of acclamation, and with one accord the delegates raised their voices in favor of Gustav. But the regent, so the reporter tells us, rose to his feet, and, mid the deafening shouts of those about him, declared that he had no wish for further honor, that he was weary of leadership, that he had found more gall than honey in the post, and that there were others more worthy than himself on whom to lay the crown. So importunate, however, were the delegates, that at last he yielded, accepted their allegiance, and took the royal oath. This done, the diet voted to levy a tax to defray the expenses of the war. Among the very first Acts to which the newly chosen monarch attached his seal was one which granted the cities of Lubeck and Dantzic, with their allies, the perpetual monopoly of all foreign trade with Sweden. At the same time it was provided that Stockholm, Kalmar, Söderköping, and Åbo should be the only ports of entry for foreign merchants in the realm. This Act was the result of an application made by Lubeck the year before, and was carried by the importunities of Lubeck's ambassadors to the diet. It was a sop to stay the flood of their demands for immediate payment of the debt incurred to Lubeck by the war. As it granted these Hanse Towns entry for all goods free of duty, it must be deemed a marked concession. One favorable clause, however, was incorporated in the Act, providing that no alien should thereafter be a burgher either of Stockholm or of Kalmar. Another measure of weight which the diet passed provided that a tax payable in silver should be levied to defray the expenses of the war, though apparently nothing was fixed by the diet as to the amount to be raised or as to the mode of levy. With this meagre record our information regarding this celebrated diet ends; but the new Cabinet, before it parted, drew up a long-winded account of the cruelties of Christiern, which it sent abroad among the people for a lasting memorial of their tyrant king.

No sooner had the diet closed its doors than the monarch sped with all the haste he could command to Stockholm. That city had been for several days in the last stages of despair. The garrison was miserably wasted in numbers, and its food was gone. Longer to look for aid from Denmark was to hope against all hope. Indeed, the wretched soldiers now thought only of the terms on which they should capitulate. During a month or more they had parleyed with their besiegers, but the terms which they had offered had thus far been refused. As soon as Gustav reached the spot, negotiations were once more opened. The new monarch, fresh from the honors of Strengnäs, seems to have shown them mercy. Apparently he granted their requests; for on the 20th of June the castle yielded, and the garrison, supplied with food and ships, set sail for Denmark. Three days later, June 23, the monarch entered the capital in triumph, amid the hosannas of his people. With this glorious issue the Swedish war of independence closed.

In contemplating this struggle as a whole, the reader will doubtless be impressed by the extraordinary ease with which the victory was won. In less than two years and a half after the first blow was struck, the

Danish tyrants had been driven from every stronghold, and the patriots had placed their leader on the throne. Indeed, eighteen months had scarcely passed when the issue was practically decided. The remaining year consisted mainly in the reduction of Sweden's strongholds, and was marked by little bloodshed. It furnished small opportunity either for brilliant strategy or for acts of startling courage. The enforced absence of the Danish monarch prevented his army from entering the field, and the patriots had neither arms nor ammunition with which to storm the forts. Both parties, therefore, waited; and the last year was little more than a test to determine the endurance of the contending armies. While, however, this period wants many of the features that make war grand, it is yet instructive if not interesting in its results. The struggle at the beginning was against overwhelming odds. The patriots had neither ammunition nor resources, and their leader was without prestige. On the other hand the Danes were well supplied with men and arms, and were led by one of the powerful monarchs of Europe backed by all the authority and influence of Rome. In spite of all this, the patriots grew in numbers day by day, while the Danish forces steadily declined. The patriots succeeded in obtaining rich supplies of men and arms from abroad, while Christiern was scarce able to keep his army from starvation. One by one the strongholds which he had seized surrendered, till finally his entire army was forced to yield, and Sweden, from her place as a weak and down-trodden Danish province, attained an enviable position among the great monarchies of Europe. The key to this marvellous transformation in the two parties can be found only in the characters of their respective leaders. The people were horrified by the brutal cruelties of Christiern, while allured by the evident sincerity and enthusiasm of Gustav. In all history there is no more striking example of the far-reaching influence which individual characters sometimes exert upon a nation's growth.

BEGINNINGS OF THE REFORMATION. 1523-1524.

WE have now reached that point in our narrative where the history of modern Sweden takes its start. With the close of the war of independence those features which mark the face of mediæval Sweden disappear, and a wholly new countenance gradually settles upon the land. Nor is this transformation peculiar in any way to Sweden. Early in the sixteenth century all Europe was passing from mediæval into modern history. In the Middle Ages there was but one criterion for every question that arose, and that criterion was the past. Whatever had been, should continue. All Church dogmas were settled by an appeal to the ancient Fathers; all political aspirations were fought out on the basis of descent. Tradition was the god of mediæval Europe. At last, however, questions arose for which tradition had no answer. On the Renaissance in Italy, on the invention of printing and of gunpowder, on the discovery of America, the ancient Fathers had not spoken. On these things, therefore, which raised the greatest questions of the age, men had nothing for it but to do their thinking for themselves. The practice thus evoked soon spread to other questions, and gradually men grew bold enough to venture opinions on certain stereotyped matters of religion. As all the world knows, the Reformation followed, and from an age of blind acceptance Europe passed to an age of eager controversy. Instead of searching to find out what had been, men argued to determine what it was desirable should be. If tradition was the characteristic of mediæval, policy is the characteristic of modern, history. Some old dogmas, like the divine right of kings, still linger; but since the fifteenth century kings have had little chance whose claims conflict with the balance of European power.

The beginnings of modern history are inextricably bound up with the beginnings of the Reformation. It is a common belief that the Reformation in Europe worked a radical change in the doctrines of religious men, raising up two parties with diametrically opposing creeds. Such a conception, however, is misleading. The Reformation was not so much a religious as a political revolt. It was the natural outcome of a growth in the power of northern Germany at a moment when Rome was losing her political prestige. The alliance between the German Empire and the popes of Rome had its origin in a need of mutual assistance. Western Europe consisted, at the accession of Charlemagne, of many independent principalities at war among themselves, and what they needed was a powerful protector to adjust their various disputes. Later this need of a protector became still more urgent, when Germany and France fell under different rulers, and the German Empire began to be threatened by the monarchy across the Rhine. Rome, by reason of her spiritual supremacy, was the arbiter to whom the northern nations naturally turned, and she found ready recompense for her services in the treasures poured generously into her lap. Such was the basis of the Holy Roman Empire. But by the beginning of the sixteenth century all this had changed. Germany was no longer weak. Her little principalities had become cemented together under an emperor well able to repel every invasion of the French. Society had made vast progress, not only in its comforts, but in its demands. Rome, on the other hand, had lost her prestige. In Italy, where the brutality and licentiousness of the popes were open to every eye, people had long since lost all reverence for the Church. This feeling did not spread readily across the Alps; but it came at last, and at a moment when Germany no longer needed aid. A nation guarded by the strong arm of Maximilian could ill brook new levies to feed the extravagance of its decrepit ally, and the infamous practices of Tetzel served as a timely pretext to shake off the burdensome alliance of the papal see. The abuses of popery were little more than a war-cry, while the real struggle of the Reformation was against the political supremacy of Rome.

In Sweden, more than in almost any other land, the Reformation was a political revolt. Indeed, it may well be called a political necessity. At the moment when Gustav Vasa was elected king, Sweden was on the verge of bankruptcy. The war just passed had drained the resources of the country, and left her heavily involved in debt. The principal creditor was Lubeck. Precisely how much had been borrowed from that town it is impossible to determine, though it is certain the total amount fell not far short of 300,000 Swedish marks. One payment of about 17,000 Swedish marks Gustav had made in 1522. This of course was a mere drop in the bucket, and other devices were necessary to relieve the general distress. One favorite device, to which allusion has been already made, consisted in a debasement of the currency. That device, however, had soon lost its savor, and the coin which in 1522 Gustav had issued for an öre and a half, he was forced in 1523 to place upon the market as an öre. So that when the new monarch ascended the throne it was manifest that the treasury must be replenished in other modes. The natural direction was that in which the greatest wealth of Sweden lay,—in other words, the Church. We have already seen how completely, in the centuries preceding the Reformation, the Church in Sweden had freed herself from all authority of the people, and had gradually accumulated for herself a vast amount of wealth. Some conception of this treasure may be had by comparing the edifices belonging to the Church with those owned by individuals. Such a comparison reveals at once an enormous disparity in favor of the Church. At a time when well-to-do citizens dwelt in what would at this day be known as hovels, they worshipped in churches that must have seemed to them palatial. The six cathedrals that existed in the time of Gustav still remain, and even at this day compare favorably with the finest structures in the land. In addition to a magnificent palace, the archbishop and the five Swedish bishops each possessed a fortified castle in his diocese. In each diocese, too, there were an enormous number of estates belonging to the bishopric; those in the diocese of Linköping, for example, numbering over six hundred. The rents and profits from these estates went directly to the bishopric, and were wholly exempt from taxation, as were also the untold treasures of gold and silver belonging to the various churches. Beside all this tithes of every species of farm produce raised in any part of Sweden were due the Church, also tithes of all other personal property acquired. Further, a small annual tax was due the Church for every building in the land from a palace to a pig-sty; also a fee for every wedding, death, or childbirth. No one could inherit property, or even take the sacrament, without a contribution to the Church. And every peasant was bound one day each year to labor for his pastor without reward. How all this money was disbursed, seems difficult to comprehend. Some clew, however, may be gained when we consider what a vast horde of clergy the Swedish people had to feed. Take, for example, the cathedrals. Most of them formed a little hierarchy in themselves. First of all was the archbishop or the bishop, who lived in regal splendor. Around him was his chapter, comprising in one instance as many as thirty canons. Then there was the archdeacon, the cantor, the scholasticus, and some thirty or forty prebends. This little army of Church officers required to be fed, and fed well—and the people of Sweden had to pay the bill. It was but natural, therefore, that, Sweden being heavily involved in debt, the monarch should seek to stay this wasteful extravagance and divert a portion of the Church incomes to the crown.

By the war of independence the way had been already paved for a war against the Church. Christiern had declared himself the champion of the pope; and the higher clergy, as vicegerents of the pope in Sweden, had generally allied themselves with the foreign party. So that the rebellion had been in large measure directed against the authorities of the Church itself, and the victory of Gustav was felt distinctly as a victory over the powers of the Church. The Chapter of Upsala had therefore deemed it policy to please Gustav, and were talking of electing his chancellor archbishop in place of Trolle, who had fled the realm. For a like reason the Chapter of Vesterås had chosen a former secretary of Sture to their vacant bishopric. The bishoprics of Strengnäs and Skara, made vacant by the expulsion of the Danes, had also been filled by persons favorable to the general policy of Gustav. So that when the new monarch assumed control, the dignitaries of the Church seemed likely to listen to his demands.

It is not for a moment to be supposed that Gustav at this time contemplated an opposition to the pope. Such an idea had been spread abroad by Christiern with a view to win sympathy in Europe; but Gustav had written to all the potentates of Europe to deny the charge, and had sent a messenger to the pope to raise a counter charge against Christiern as the murderer of two Swedish bishops in the slaughter of 1520. The pope, already distrustful of his Danish ally, had listened favorably to the message, and in the following summer, 1523, had sent a legate to Sweden to inform him further on the subject.

This papal legate, Johannes Magni, was the son of a pious burgher of Linköping, and along with his two brothers had been educated from childhood for the Church. At the age of eighteen so marvellous was his precocity that he was made a canon both of Linköping and of Skara. Later, as was the practice with scholars of that period, he continued his studies at several of the leading universities in Europe. But in spite of a sojourn of some seventeen years away from Sweden, he never ceased to keep up a fervid interest in the affairs of his native land. As soon as the atrocities of Christiern reached his ears, he made a personal visit to Pope Leo X. and denounced the practices of the Danish king. The suggestions which he offered seem to have been scorned by Leo; but in 1521 that pontiff died, and his successor, Adrian VI., listened more readily to the Swedish canon. Adrian himself was from the north of Europe, and had earlier been an instructor of Johannes in the University of Louvain. The characters of the two were not unlike. Both held strong theological opinions, and looked with dread upon all opposition to the papal power. But they were both keenly alive to the abuses that had gathered about the Church, and were eager to repress them. Johannes was peculiarly suited by nature for a work of compromise. With no ordinary talents, of untiring energy, sympathetic, generous, and conciliating, but withal imbued with an ardent love of the Church, Adrian at once discerned in him a valuable mediator. When, therefore, Gustav wrote to Rome to defend himself against the charge of heresy, the pope selected Johannes as his legate, with instructions to proceed to Sweden and investigate the charges made against each other by Christiern and Gustav. The legate, complying with these orders, arrived in Sweden while the diet of Strengnäs was in session. He therefore made his way directly to that town. While on the road the tidings reached him that Gustav Vasa had been elected king. As soon as the new monarch learned of his approach, he sent for him to come before the house. There he was overwhelmed with expressions of gratitude for his past interest in the Swedish cause. In return the legate addressed the house at great length in favor of Gustav. The impression left upon his hearers was so pleasing that the Cabinet drew up a letter to the pope requesting that Johannes be given full authority, with the bishops of Sweden, to reform the Swedish Church. In the same letter opportunity was taken to denounce the vices of Archbishop Trolle, and to beg that, he having already resigned and fled the kingdom, the pope should use his authority to have a new archbishop chosen in his stead.

This document bears strong evidence of the influence of the king. Its allusion to the resignation of Archbishop Trolle was of course untrue. That prelate had fled the realm to escape the fury of his opponents, but he still looked for the restoration of Danish power and a return of his own prerogatives in the Swedish Church. The king's desire, as reflected in the letter of his Cabinet, was to secure from the pope a recognition that the archbishopric was vacant, and then to use this recognition to force the unwilling Chapter of Upsala to nominate as archbishop one who was in the interests of the king. The scheme, however, failed; for Pope Adrian died before he had had time to act, and was succeeded by a pontiff who hated everything which savored of reform.

During the first months of his reign Gustav was made wretched by the importunate demands of Lubeck. Her ambassadors continually dogged his steps, and declared they would not leave him till every cent that Sweden owed was paid. After the fall of Kalmar the monarch needed his foreign mercenaries no longer, and would gladly have cashiered them and sent them off. But the "klippings" struck the year before had so far lost the confidence of his subjects that the soldiers refused to take them at any price at all, and Gustav was compelled to keep his men on foot till he could obtain the silver requisite to issue better coins. The diet just dissolved had passed an act providing for the levy of new taxes to be paid in silver, and the king apparently had been given power to fix the mode in which the levy should be made. This was a matter which required skilful handling; and it is fair to say that the policy which the king pursued, if not perfectly straightforward, showed, at any rate, rare skill. Fearing lest another direct call upon the peasantry would raise an outcry, he resolved to make his application to the Church, and give her the option of surrendering a portion of her riches or of losing her prestige by laying new burdens on her devotees. With this in view he wrote first of all to Brask, and after demanding some five thousand guilders which he understood that prelate had stored away in Lubeck, he called upon him to collect four hundred marks in silver from the clergy of his diocese. He then issued a proclamation to the churches and monasteries throughout the land to send him all the chalices, patens, and ornaments that could be spared from the altars, as well as all the silver coin that could be found; and along with this he published a statement of the total amount which each diocese and monastery must provide. Two things are noticeable in this proclamation: first, it does not specify the amount which each particular church must furnish; and, secondly, it distinctly states that the sums handed over are to be deemed as loans, which he will duly acknowledge and ultimately pay in full. In his letter to Brask, on the contrary, the exact amount for which the bishop must be responsible is named, and no definite promise is given to repay it. The document seems part of a deliberate plan to crush the power of the crafty bishop. This Brask noticed, and in his reply adverted to a suspicion lest for some reason he had incurred the king's displeasure, which he would willingly avert. The simplest mode of averting the king's displeasure would have been a speedy compliance with the king's demand. For this, however, Brask had little relish. So Gustav, two weeks later, wrote again. "We are much surprised," he said, "that you show no more concern while a weight like this rests upon the kingdom. The amount which we must raise without a moment's delay is two hundred thousand guilders, and the Lubeck ambassadors refuse point-blank to depart unless they take that sum with them. If they don't get it we fear open war, which God forbid! Therefore, by the allegiance which you owe us and the realm, we exhort you, send the four hundred marks' weight without delay." Even this appeal had no immediate effect, and after two weeks more he sent Brask another despatch. "The Lubeck ambassadors," wrote the king, "will not leave us till they get the money which we owe in Lubeck,—a vast sum. It is, therefore, of necessity that we lay this tax upon the churches and monasteries. Strain every nerve to obtain some relief for us in your diocese, especially from your churches and monasteries; the clergy we shall spare for the present." The bishop finally complied, though with an ill grace; and on the 10th of August we find Gustav writing that he has so far satisfied the demands of Lubeck that her ambassadors have parted from him on good terms.

The tax had been collected, though not without much friction. It had found the people in an irritable temper, and it had left them more irritable still. The ruin which the war had caused was visible on every hand, and the blessings that were expected to follow were not so easily discerned.

During two years the fields had been lying fallow, commerce had steadily declined, and the people were actually suffering for food. Stockholm had been rendered desolate. Its population had fallen to about one quarter. "Every other house," wrote Gustav, "is now empty;" and there appeared so little chance of a revival that the king issued a proclamation calling on the burghers of other towns as far as possible to sell their houses and settle down in Stockholm. Another cause of dissatisfaction was that, though the war was over in Sweden, the Swedish possessions in Finland were still in the hands of the enemy, and a considerable army was needed to reduce them. Fredrik, king of Denmark, had resigned his claim to Sweden; but certain islands off the coast, as well as some districts along the frontier of Norway, were still matters of dispute. All these circumstances tended to raise a spirit of discontent, which, though for the nonce restrained, was ready to break out into violence at any moment. To prevent evil, Gustav resolved to issue a proclamation to the people.

On the 8th of September the annual fair at Vesterås was opened, and Gustav seized this opportunity to make a public statement of his doings. This statement was in the nature of an apology for the recent tax. It declared in the first place that the expenses of the war had reached a higher figure than had ever been incurred by Swedish king before, amounting to a total of over nine hundred thousand marks. A large part of this sum was for foreign troops, hired that the Swedish peasantry might "stay at home in peace, tending their fields and pastures, and caring for their wives and children." When the war was over and the mercenaries were ready to depart, they had demanded with threats of violence immediate payment for all the arms and vessels they had furnished. Having no means to satisfy them, Gustav had consulted with his Cabinet, and by their advice had called upon the churches and monasteries for a loan, "which with God's help shall be paid, if all goes well." "Nor," continued the monarch, "was this tax in any way a departure from the practice of former rulers, as may be seen by referring to the ancient records.... Some there are among you who assert openly or in private that we have fleeced the churches and monasteries. This we assert distinctly we have not done, but have merely called upon them for a loan, which shall be paid.... We trust you will give no heed to such conspirators and traitors, but will aid us in bringing them to punishment." The document closes with some remarks upon the coinage. "It must be clear to all," it runs, "that with the enormous expenses which have been rolling up against us we could not issue coins of the quality which you are accustomed to of old. From sheer necessity we have issued 'klippings' after the pattern of King Christiern, though his coins are now, thank God! departed from the realm.... These 'klippings' are at present not accepted for more than half their worth; and while this has been strenuously forbidden, the only result thus far has been that traders have refused to trade at all, and have carried their salt and hops and clothing back to Germany. We therefore intend at the first opportunity to instruct our Cabinet with the most learned men of the various classes to determine whether the 'klippings' shall be accepted for their present value or for less; and whatever their decision, we promise faithfully we shall obey."

After administering this soothing drug, the monarch turned his thoughts once more to the appointment of a new archbishop. The letter despatched by the Cabinet to Pope Adrian immediately after the diet of Strengnäs had proved of little service, for Brask on the 18th of July had secretly sent a messenger to the pope with word that Church property was being confiscated. Gustav, ignorant of the bishop's perfidy and wondering at the pope's delay, now wrote again. "For a long time, Holy Father," began the courteous monarch, "our cathedral chapters have urged us to solicit you in behalf of the persons elected by them to fill their vacant posts. Trolle having resigned the archbishopric, the prelates and canons of Upsala have chosen your legate Johannes Magni in his stead; the canons of Skara have chosen their archdeacon Magnus Haraldsson to the bishopric vacated by his predecessor's death; and the canons of Strengnäs have chosen their provost Magnus Sommar. The prelates and canons of Vesterås, their bishop having died, present the name of Petrus Magni for the post. In Åbo, though the bishop died a year ago, no successor has as yet been chosen, that church having only recently been captured from our enemies. As the persons above named are satisfactory to us and to our people, we beg you to confirm them as soon as possible, and thus avert the danger to which vacancies in the episcopal office would expose the Church." Whether or not the Chapters had actually elected all the persons named, may well be doubted, and is, indeed, of little moment; for their spirit was by this time broken, and if they cherished any preferences they dared not speak them. The letter was intrusted to Johannes Magni with orders to obtain confirmation from the pope and then return to Sweden. But just as he was making ready to depart, the long-awaited letter came from Adrian, though it differed much in tenor from what had been expected. Instead of urging the Upsala Chapter to choose a new archbishop, it commanded Gustav to restore Archbishop Trolle to his post, threatening him with punishment if he refused.

This change of colors on the part of Adrian has been accounted for in many ways. Johannes Magni himself suggested that it was the work of evil-minded counsellors in Rome. The more probable supposition is that Adrian had been influenced by Brask. If Church property was being confiscated, as Brask declared, Archbishop Trolle could be relied on to offer much more strenuous resistance than the prelate talked of as his successor. But the very reason which induced the pope to favor Trolle seemed to the king sufficient ground for supporting his opponent. It was precisely because of Johannes Magni's pliable and compromising temper that Gustav would have rejoiced to see the mitre on his head. He was determined that Trolle, at any rate, should not wear it. So he sat down, as soon as Adrian's letter came, and wrote a warm reply to the College of Cardinals in Rome. "If our Most Holy Father," he said, "has any care for the peace of our country, we shall be pleased to have him confirm the election of his legate Johannes to the archbishopric, and we shall comply with the pope's wishes as to a reformation of the Christian Church and religion. But if his Holiness, against our honor and the peace of our subjects, sides with the crime-stained partisans of Archbishop Trolle, we shall allow his legate to return to Rome, and shall govern the Church in this country with the authority which we have as king, and in a manner which we believe will please God as well as all the princes of Christendom. We beg you, however, to use your authority in the Apostolic See in such way as not to harm our state, nor give the appearance of championing the crimes of Trolle against the tranquillity of a Christian people." Three days after writing this vehement despatch, the monarch sent off another, couched in language even more determined, to the pope. "We shall never," he declared, "allow that man to return as our archbishop. He not only is unworthy of the priesthood, he is unworthy even to live. We respect the Roman Church, and if need be would die in her behalf. But if she endeavors thus to ruin our country, we shall resist her till the last drop of blood is shed." This document was placed in the hands of Olaus Magni, brother of the proposed archbishop, with orders to inform the pope of the evils to which the Church in Sweden was exposed, and to use his utmost endeavor to secure the confirmation of the bishops. The missive, however, never reached the pontiff to whom it was addressed. Adrian was already dead and buried ere the document was penned; and when the messenger arrived in Rome, he found another pontiff, Clement VII., seated in the papal chair.

The breach between the king and popery was now open. Gustav had actually flung down the gauntlet at the feet of Rome, asserting that if officers satisfactory to him were not appointed by the pope, he would take the duty of appointing them upon himself. Still he did not relinquish hope that the breach might yet be healed; and on the 2d of November he wrote again, this time requesting the pope to confirm the election of Erik Svensson, a former secretary of Gustav, to the vacant bishopric of Åbo. "And if your Holiness," wrote the king, "shall delay in confirming the bishops-elect, we shall ourselves undertake the restoration of our ruined churches, and shall have the bishops confirmed by Him who is our High Pontifex, that His Church and religion may not be injured through the negligence of the Apostolic See. Moreover, Most Holy Father, we hear from certain men of Lubeck that one Francisco of Potentia has returned from Rome to Denmark with arguments in justification of that tyrant Christiern's massacre of our bishops, and that your Holiness has rewarded him with the bishopric of Skara. If this be true, the Apostolic See has done us and the Church a wrong equal in enormity to that of the Danish king, and we shall by God's aid avert it if necessary with our blood. Let not your Holiness fancy that we shall permit foreigners to rule the Church in Sweden." At about the same time with this letter the monarch, in writing to Johannes Magni, uses even stronger language. After suggesting that Christiern has so impoverished the Church that it is unable to send its bishops elect to Rome for confirmation, he asserts that it is rumored the real cause of the delay is that the Church has not been able to furnish the pope the customary fees for confirmation. "Some assert, too," he adds, "that there is no authority in Scripture for all the dues that belong by custom to the pope.... So soon as we find that our patience and moderation are of no avail, we shall proceed to rigorous measures. We shall not suffer our people to bend beneath a cruel foreign yoke, for we are confident that Christ, who is our High Priest, will not let his people die to suit the pope's caprice."

These were bold words to use of the potentate whose command all Christendom obeyed. The youthful monarch, it was already clear, intended to rule his country with an iron hand. When only three months on the throne, he chanced upon some letters in which the bishop of Vesterås alluded to him in arrogant and contumelious terms. This bishop, who gloried in the name of Peder Sunnanväder, had been at one time chancellor of the young Sten Sture, and though elected in 1522 to the bishopric of Vesterås, had suffered the same fate as the other bishops and never been confirmed. Gustav did not hesitate a moment. As soon as the abusive letters reached him, he proceeded with the entire Cabinet to Vesterås, and summoned the bishop with all his canons to the chapter-house. There he laid before them the evidences of the bishop's guilt. Unable to furnish satisfactory explanation, the bishop was removed; and the Chapter, at the instance of Gustav, elected Petrus Magni in his stead. Even with this, however, the monarch's vengeance did not end. Knut, the dean of Vesterås and a former chancellor of Gustav,—the man, indeed, who had been talked of for the archbishopric of Upsala,—was indiscreet enough to come forward at the trial with an apology for his bishop. The monarch wanted no other proof of his complicity, and discharged him along with Sunnanväder from his post.

Gustav was spurred on in his campaign against the Church by a continued need of money to keep his army in the field. Even after the subjection of Sweden he had to carry on the war in Finland; and it was not till nearly Christmas, and after he had sent a strong force of mercenaries across the Baltic, that Finland was subdued. After this the great bone of contention was the isle of Gotland. This island, or rather its capital, the town of Visby, had been in ages past the leader of the Hanseatic League. Its situation in the Baltic, not far from the east coast of southern Sweden, made it still of great value to merchant-vessels passing between Sweden and the Hanseatic Towns. When Christiern fled from Denmark, Gotland was under the control of Norby, who continued after his master's fall to make depredations along the coast of Sweden and seize all merchantmen that came within his grasp. Danish, Swedish, and Hanse vessels were alike his prey, till Gotland came to be known by all as a "nest of robbers." Fredrik and Lubeck, unwilling though they were that Gotland should fall to Sweden, welcomed any movement intended to root out this impediment to the Baltic trade, and raised no opposition when Gustav offered, in the winter of 1524, to attack the island in the coming spring. The attitude of Fredrik to Gustav recalls the fable of the monkey and the cat. The Danish king hoped ultimately to secure the chestnuts for himself, but in the mean time was not sorry to see an army gathering in Sweden to bear the brunt of the assault. Which party first proposed an expedition against Gotland is not clear. At the general diet held in Vadstena in January, representatives from Fredrik were present, and it was agreed that the expedition should be made as soon as the harbors opened. The quotas to be furnished by the different parts of Sweden by the first week after Easter were also fixed. The Danish envoys, it appears, made no promises except that a congress of the two realms should be held on the 14th of February to settle all matters of dispute. The passports for the Danish envoys to this convention were issued by Gustav on the spot. They were never used, however; for just before the appointed day he received notice from the Danish Cabinet that they wished the congress to be postponed. This action caused Brask to suspect that Fredrik's sole object was to use up time. Whatever Fredrik's object, the congress could not be held without him. Gustav therefore postponed it till the end of April, and set about raising an army for himself.

The first person to whom the monarch turned was Bishop Brask. It appears that there had been some dispute between the bishop and one of the hospitals in his diocese as to the tithes from certain lands. The shrewd monarch conceived the notion that the simplest mode of settling the dispute was to hand the disputed property over to the crown. He wrote, therefore, to both parties to send him at once the original documents on which they based their claims. "And meantime," he said, "we forbid you positively to collect the disputed tithes. Should you touch them, we shall be forced to take further steps. We have, indeed, been told that in the times of our fathers the crown received from the canons throughout the realm one fourth of their tithes under the name of 'the poor man's portion,' with the understanding that the money should be used to found hospitals, and over these hospitals the crown has ever since held *jus patronatus.*" To this demand Brask answered that he would send the documents desired, but that the crown had never taken the tithes from the canons except by force. A few weeks later, on the 18th of February, the king wrote Brask that the expedition would start as soon as the harbors opened, and that, as Brask had been one of the promoters of the scheme, he must expect to contribute generously toward it, especially since he and his diocese, being nearest to the isle of Gotland, would be the ones most benefited by the overthrow of Norby. Brask, in his answer of March 8, repudiated the idea that the expedition was the fruit of his brain, and expressed the hope that the matter might be settled without bloodshed. "'T is never wise," he said, "to break down doors already open." Brask asserted, further, that he had never received a penny of rent from Gotland, but promised to do all he could to obtain aid from the churches of his diocese.

By this time it had become rumored that the king was about to levy a new tax upon the people, and a murmur of discontent had risen through the land. To allay this, Gustav issued several letters, declaring that the contribution was to be wholly voluntary. One of the convents he begged to send him all the silver collected for a certain shrine, and offered to give the crown's note for the amount, secured, if the convent wished it, by a mortgage of certain crown fiefs. In writing to the people of Östergötland he pointed out that the expedition was necessitated by the piracies of Norby, who had caused a dreadful scarcity of food by checking imports; and he called upon the people to have a detachment of armed men ready by the first week after Easter at the latest, promising at the same time that as soon as the fleet should put to sea the men would be provided for at the crown's expense. To the people of Brask's diocese he wrote that he had heard a rumor to the effect that he was imposing a new tax upon the people. This rumor the king characterized as "a palpable lie." He declared further that he had applied the crown rents to pay for the expedition, and had asked their bishop to make a loan from his rents for the same purpose, to which Brask had replied that he would lend the money, but would raise it by imposing a tax upon his churches. This Gustav declared was not his desire; all he wished was a free-will offering. From this letter it is clear the monarch sought to cast upon Brask the odium which this new levy had brought upon himself, and it is equally clear that in doing so he exceeded the bounds of truth. In calling upon Brask for a contribution he had in no way specified the mode in which the money should be raised; and Brask, so far from refusing to apply his own rents for the purpose, haddistinctly stated, in every letter which he wrote, that he would do his utmost to furnish the desired sum.

A further cause of disaffection lay in the general impression that the monarch was tampering with the coinage. This impression had its origin naturally enough in the fact that the general diet held in January had repudiated the Swedish "klippings." The reason given for that act was that, the Danish "klippings" having been repudiated in Denmark the year before, merchants were bringing barrelfuls of them into Sweden; so that the Swedish "klipping," being scarcely discernible from its Danish namesake, fell constantly in value, its fluctuations depending upon the importations of the repudiated coin from Denmark. In the Act repudiating the Swedish "klipping" that coin was declared to be worth four "hvitar;" that is, about one half of the amount which the crown had received in issuing it. The outcry which this Act called forth was universal, and the king was forced to issue a letter to the people in which he endeavored to allay their wrath. "We have never," he declared with brazen falsehood,—"we have never altered the coinage either by raising or by lowering its value, but have permitted each coin to pass for the same value as it had before;" and he added with bland simplicity, "the coin has fallen by its own weight." The striking feature in this matter is the audacity of the king. He trusted that the people generally would not have access to the documents which we now possess to contradict him. After issuing this mendacious letter, he approached the Stockholm merchants, and, by certain persuasive arguments whose nature it is easy to conceive, prevailed upon them to deposit all their "klippings" in the treasury, to be weighed and bought by the Government at their actual bullion value. He then began the issue of a new series of coins approximating though still below their face value, and published another letter, this time acknowledging that he had repudiated the "klippings," but asserting that the step was taken to comply with a suggestion made him by the people.

Late in March Gustav received a note from Fredrik requesting a further postponement of the congress till May 15. As the Vend Cities were to be present, Gustav answered that he would communicate with Lubeck, and so soon as he had word from her would give a definite reply. He then despatched the Danish monarch's letter to Bishop Brask. The answer of that prelate was full of wisdom. "I marvel much," wrote Brask, "that his Grace should call a congress of these three realms without first consulting you.... He must be well aware that you cannot be present on so short notice, especially since he knows that you are about to make an expedition against Gotland. His real purpose, I suspect, is to induce you to postpone your expedition." In this surmise the shrewd bishop doubtless was correct. Fredrik, though satisfied that Sweden should go to great expense in preparing for an expedition against Gotland, was reluctant to see her armies actually land upon the isle, lest his own claims to Gotland might thereby be lost. It seemed to him that Norby, terrified by the armaments of Sweden, might be induced to go to Denmark and yield the isle to him. He therefore wrote to Sweden, requesting that the pirate be given a safe-conduct through the land. But the army was already in the field, and Gustav answered firmly that he would not comply with the request. To this answer he was induced partly by a suspicion that Denmark was already furnishing supplies to Norby.

On the 8th of May Gustav despatched his fleet, eight thousand strong, to Gotland. The command he gave to a German adventurer who has already figured in this story as Berent von Mehlen. This person, after breaking faith with his former master, Christiern, had married a cousin of Gustav, and had become a trusted counsellor of the king. By what traits he became attractive in his monarch's eyes it is at this day difficult to conceive. Certainly as a general he knew as little as any general possibly could know. Again and again he had been given opportunity to display his warlike power, but thus far in every instance he had failed. He now set forth, as admiral of the Swedish fleet, to besiege the town of Visby. The siege began on the 19th of May, and was enlivened during a few weeks by several skirmishes. Nothing of importance, however, was accomplished. The siege was protracted through the summer, and at last the besiegers showed so little life that their leader, the favorite of Gustav, was reported to have turned his coat once more and joined the enemy.

Not yet had the siege begun when evidence was furnished that Fredrik was in league with Norby. So early as the 9th of May Gustav wrote to Brask that the Danes were rumored to be supplying Norby with stores and ammunition. A few days later word arrived from Fredrik that he wished once more to put off the congress, this time till the 24th of June. Gustav was now fairly mad with indignation, and declared to Brask that he would neither be present nor allow his envoys to be present at the proposed congress. He was discreet enough, however, to conceal his wrath from Fredrik; and, without refusing the offer of the Danish king, he called a meeting of his Cabinet, to which he urged Lubeck to send her envoys. Fredrik in the mean time had been negotiating on his own account with Norby, and had wrung promises from him which led to the impression that Norby had thrown up his allegiance to Christiern II. and was ready to accept the authority of Fredrik. Elated by this false hope, the Danish monarch felt in a position to ignore the slight that had been put upon him by Gustav, and sent delegates, apparently unbidden, to the Swedish king and Cabinet, proposing that a congress be held in Denmark to settle all matters of dispute, the Swedish army in the mean time to withdraw from Gotland, and Norby to be given safe-conduct from the isle. These terms Gustav rejected with disdain, declaring that he had striven for the good of all to scatter Norby with his "nest of robbers," and would consent to a meeting with Fredrik only on condition that in the interval Norby should receive no aid of any shape or kind. Fredrik, finding that Gustav was determined, and that Norby's feigned alliance was somewhat airy, yielded reluctantly to this condition. The Swedish army continued in its camp at Visby; and the two monarchs, attended by their Cabinets, proceeded to the town of Malmö in hope of settling their disputes. The congress opened on the first day of September. The two monarchs with their retinues were present, together with envoys from the Hanseatic Towns. The meeting opened, as was usual, with an interchange of courtesies and with mutual promises to resist their common enemy, King Christiern. It was agreed, too, that all renegades from either country should be returned, and that citizens of one country should be entitled to any property belonging to them in the other. As soon, however, as the question of disputed territory arose, it became clear that no conclusion could be reached. It was therefore resolved, after long debate, that this question be postponed, to be decided by a congress of certain Hanse Towns, to be held in Lubeck in June of the following year. Till then a provisional frontier agreed upon by Norway, Denmark, and Sweden was to be observed; and Gotland was to remain during the interval in the hands of that party which held it on September 1. If it should be found that Norby held it on that day, he should be called upon to surrender it to Fredrik, to be placed by him under the temporary control of some person satisfactory to Sweden, Denmark, and Lubeck. If Sweden should continue the war in Gotland, she was to pay for all damage she might do. Either party by violating these terms was to become indebted to the other to the amount of one hundred thousand guilders. This conclusion reached, the congress was dissolved, envoys being first sent to Gotland to carry out the terms. Finding that Norby was still in possession, they entered into negotiations, and soon obtained a contract, signed by Norby as well as Mehlen, that each should withdraw his forces from the land. In conformity with this contract Mehlen at once broke camp and sailed with all the Swedish fleet to Kalmar; but Norby, laughing at the credulity of his opponent, continued to dominate the island, and began his piracies afresh.

This disastrous expedition caused a heavy drain upon the Swedish treasury, an evil which the monarch sought to meet by new demands upon the Church. On the 9th of May he wrote to Brask that he must have more money, and that the bishopric of Linköping, being benefited more than others by the expedition, must expect to bear the chief part of the cost. To this Brask answered humbly that he had already furnished more than his proper share, but would do his utmost to obtain the needed sum. This promise, however, did not satisfy the king; and a few days later he sent a letter to Brask's chapter, declaring that they had collected certain rents belonging to the crown which must be yielded up without delay. Brask appears to have been a special object of the monarch's greed. On one occasion Gustav seized some tithes belonging to that prelate, and then had face enough to write him that he had done so, his only excuse being that the army was in need of food. This high-handed mode of dealing with the Church is in marked contrast to the monarch's complaisance when dealing with the people. Before the common people Gustav grovelled in the dust. Every day nearly he despatched some document granting new privileges to this town or to that; and when the people of Kalmar refused to contribute on the ground that their trade had been ruined by foreign merchants, Gustav sent back answer that he would remedy this wrong. The notion getting abroad in Brask's diocese that new taxes were being levied, Gustav insisted that the bishop should counteract this view, thus practically forcing him to make the contribution from his private means.

In spite of every effort to appease the people, discontent was fast spreading through the land. To attribute this entirely to the actions of Gustav is unfair. His expedition against Gotland, it is true, had proved a failure, and had cost his country dear. The monarch should have seen that, in the impoverished state of his finances, the duty of destroying Norby belonged to Denmark or Lubeck. But, granted that the expedition was ill-judged, its failure certainly did not justify revolt. The truth is, the Swedish people were so used to insurrection that the slightest disappointment sufficed to set the whole country by the ears, and no sooner was the expedition brought to its humiliating end than the people began to look about for pretexts for revolt. One of the first cries raised against Gustav was that he had transgressed the law by admitting foreign citizens into the Cabinet of Sweden. To this charge the monarch was unable to make a rational reply. At the very outset of his reign, he had displayed his first infatuation for foreign men by raising Mehlen to the highest honors of the state. Later another adventurer, one Count Johan von Hoya, had appeared upon the scene. The king had forthwith showered royal favors upon his head. Scarcely two months after landing Hoya had betrothed himself to the king's sister, and had been received by the infatuated monarch into the Swedish Cabinet. Such a course appeared to the people in direct opposition to the promise made by Gustav that he would drive out foreign power. This evil, however, was but slight, in comparison with others that the people had to bear. In plain English, they were starving. The long-protracted war with Denmark, followed by the brutal piracies of Norby, had so reduced the supply of necessaries, particularly salt, that few except the rich were able to get enough to stay their hunger. Hoping to allay the people's indignation in these matters, Gustav called a meeting of his Cabinet in October, summoning at the same time two Linköping burghers to advise the Cabinet as to the best methods of improving trade. It is worthy of note, however, that though the meeting was expressly announced to be called for the purpose of improving trade, the documents describing the debate are devoted almost wholly to a consideration of methods to augment the royal funds. The king, it seems, came forward with a suggestion that, since he was likely soon to marry, some, provision should be made for adding to his income, and some steps be taken to reimburse him for the sums advanced by him to carry on the war. What he particularly wanted was the right to fix, according to his own judgment, the amount of rents to be paid by crown estates. He suggested, further, that, since the pope would not confirm the bishops till they paid their fees, his coronation should be delayed no longer, but the bishops should perform the ceremony without the papal sanction. He recommended also that, there being no satisfactory place in which to keep the Swedish cavalry, they be quartered in the various monasteries, "where," he added, "we find plenty of money, but very few monks." As to Hoya, he requested the Cabinet's sanction of the proposed marriage, shrewdly intimating that while he favored citizens of Germany, he believed no marriage between a Swede and Dane should be allowed. The answer which the Cabinet made to these proposals shows traces of a feeble opposition along with a manifest endeavor to accommodate the king. First of all, the Cabinet advised the king to appoint a few of the most intelligent and able debaters in the realm to represent the cause of Sweden at the congress to be held next year in Lubeck; and in accordance with this suggestion the king named Hoya, and the new archbishop, Johannes Magni. Regarding the matter of conferring fiefs on Hoya, the Cabinet yielded to the king's desire. "Though the law declares," they said, "that no foreigner shall enter the Cabinet or govern land or castle, yet we shall gladly see you grant him both castle and land as you deem best, doubting not that you will so watch over his and all other grants that your subjects suffer not." In accordance with this concession Hoya was given Stegeborg in fee, and his marriage with Margareta was arranged to take place in January next. As to quartering in the monasteries, the conservative element prevailed, the Cabinet decreeing that it was not advisable to fill the monasteries with horse and men. That the coronation take place at once, the Cabinet strongly urged, though they refrained from expressing opinion as to the confirmation of the bishops. The proposition that the king be given power to regulate the royal rents was not rejected, but a hint was thrown out that the proper step was rather to prepare an accurate list of all crown property and collect the rents as due thereon of old.

Clearly enough this meeting would not satisfy a hungry people. In fact apparently it added to their rage, and we find the people of Dalarne at this time drawing up a long list of grievances to be laid before the king. Their first and weightiest complaint was that certain rich men, stewards of the king, had bought up all the grain in their district, and had made a corner in it so that the poor man could not get enough to eat. Further than this, they protested against the king's practice of admitting into the kingdom all sorts of foreigners, "who have put their heads together to ruin the common people." This vehement lament aroused Gustav to the gravity of his position, particularly as he learned that Sunnanväder was inciting the people to rebel. Hoping to quiet matters, he despatched his messengers to all parts of the kingdom with soothing words. He endeavored in every way to impress upon the people that the high price of food was due entirely to the war between the emperor and the King of France; and as to the repudiation of the "klippings," of which some people had complained, he asserted that he had thereby suffered far greater injury than his people. Sunnanväder's conspiracy was the thing that caused him most anxiety, and on the 9th of December he addressed the Dalesmen on that theme. "Dear friends," he suavely wrote, "report has reached our ears that Sunnanväder has gone among you with plots to throw the kingdom into strife once more. We beg you in the name of God give him no heed. He has made statements about us, we are told, which are absolutely false; among others, that we are about to restore Trolle to his archbishopric,—the man who deprived us of father and mother and threw our kingdom into ruin. As we have called a diet to be held in January, to investigate these charges among other things, we request you at that time or earlier to send representatives from every parish to judge between us; and we hereby promise the said Sunnanväder safe-conduct to and from Stockholm for this investigation. You may make this proclamation to him; and if he will not come, you may know that he is false.... Further, since we are informed that you are suffering from great lack of salt, we have just despatched to you between ten and twenty cargoes of salt to relieve your want."

While Gustav was thus dickering with the Dalesmen, a far more weighty matter kept him continually on an anxious seat at home. This was the Reformation of the Romish Church. It has been already noted that the Swedish Reformation was a political revolt, and at its outset had but little connection with theological dispute. The conflagration that had raged in Germany since 1519 produced no immediate effect in Sweden, and it was not till the spring of 1523 that the Swedish prelates felt real dread of Martin Luther. The father of the Swedish Reformation was Olaus Petri, a blacksmith's son, of Örebro. From his earliest years this champion of Luther had been educated by a pious father for the Romish Church. His childhood had been passed amid the religious influence of a monastery in his native town. There, with his younger brother Laurentius, he had shared the daily routine of a monk. When a mere boy his father, little knowing the temptation to which his son would be exposed, had placed him in the University of Wittenberg, where he sat for some years at the feet of Luther. On his return to Sweden in 1519, he was appointed to give instructions in the Bible to the youth of Strengnäs. Though only twenty-two, he already showed such promise that within a year he was chosen deacon of Strengnäs, and placed at the head of the school belonging to the Chapter. The opportunity thus given him was great. The bishopric being vacant, the charge of things in Strengnäs fell upon Laurentius Andreæ, at the time archdeacon. Andreæ, though fifteen years his senior, was of a kindred spirit, and by a contemporary is described as a willing pupil of the young reformer. There can be no question that even at this period Petri was regarded as a man of strength. A portrait of him painted when still a youth shows in a marked degree the traits by which he was distinguished later. The face is full and round, with large, warm eyes twinkling with merriment, and a high, clear forehead, from which is thrown back a heavy mass of waving hair. The mouth is firm as adamant, and the sharp-cut lips and chin are eloquent of strength. Altogether, it is the picture of just the man that Petri afterward became,—a brilliant orator, daring, good-natured, and gifted with a generous supply of common-sense. Precisely how much Petri owed to Martin Luther we cannot know. It is not, however, likely that at first his teaching in Strengnäs differed materially from that inculcated by the Romish Church. At any rate, he taught four years before any serious complaint was made. The first to charge him with heresy was Bishop Brask. On the 7th of May, 1523, that much-enduring prelate wrote to a member of the Upsala Chapter that a certain person in Strengnäs had inflamed the people by preaching heresies; "and God knows," he added, "we are grieved enough to learn that he is not silenced." What these heresies preached by Petri were, appears from a polemic hurled at the young reformer by Brask's deacon. They include, among other things, a denial of the priest's authority to solicit alms, with assertions that men should place no faith in the Virgin or in other saints, but in God alone; that the priest's first duty is to preach, not pray, and that confession should be made to none but God. Surely we have here the very essence of the Reformation. Brask was already trembling with apprehension, and despatched a letter to a brother bishop to say that the heresies of Petri had begun to break out in Upsala. "We must use our utmost vehemence," he gasped, "to persuade Johannes Magni to apply the inquisition to this Petri; otherwise the flame will spread throughout the land." Magni, it is clear, was deemed a little lukewarm by such ardent men as Brask, and on the 12th of July we find Brask pouring out a flood of Latin eloquence to excite the tranquil legate. In nothing is Brask's sagacity more manifest than in the enthusiasm which he here displayed. He discerned with perfect clearness that the battle must be fought at once. If Petri should once gain the people's ear, all hope was lost. Romanism was no match for Lutheranism in an open war. He therefore sought to stamp out the new teachings without allowing them to be fairly known; and had his superiors shown equal zeal, the Reformation might have been delayed.

A few days after his earnest appeal to Magni, Brask despatched to the Vadstena Chapter a tract in refutation of the Lutheran doctrines, and along with it a sermon preached by Petri, "in which," so wrote the bishop, "you will observe his blasphemy of the Holy Virgin." Brask, despite his spiritual duties, was no ascetic, and, though suffering at the time from illness, added a postscript begging the Chapter to let him have a box of nuts. Apparently these delicacies came; for the bishop's next letter, written to the pope, was in a happier vein. "I have just had from Johannes Magni a letter on exterminating heresy which fills my soul with joy.... I grieve, however, to tell you that the heresy which had its birth in Germany has spread its branches across this kingdom.... I have sought to the utmost of my power to stay the pestilence, but through lack of authority outside my diocese, could not accomplish what I would.... Give me your orders to act outside my diocese, and I will crush the heresy with my utmost zeal." About this time the bishop received a letter from Johannes Magni that must have soothed his temper. "God knows," the legate wrote, "how eagerly I burn to effect the hoped-for freedom of the Christian Church, had not circumstances been adverse. I have at any rate pleaded with the king, and he has promised to maintain our rights. He says that if any of his soldiers wrong our tenants, they do so at their peril. When I spoke to him of the burdens that had been put upon us, he exclaimed with tears in his eyes that no one felt it more than he, that it had been necessary and contrary to his will, and that it was his full intention so soon as peace was restored to refund the money we had furnished. He promised also to repress the Lutheran heresy, though he urged me to use persuasion rather than force, lest by conflict of opinions the whole Church be overturned." The impression left on Magni by his monarch's tears is probably the impression that the monarch had designed. We have no reason to suppose Gustav cherished any affection yet for Luther, but neither is there reason to suppose he hated him. What he hoped for above all else was to keep the bishops under his control, and the surest way to do so was to keep the Church at enmity with Luther.

That Gustav played his cards with skill is manifest from a letter written by Magni to the Linköping Chapter. "I understand," he wrote, "that you feel little anxiety at my proposed return to Rome, thinking that I have not shown enough energy in restoring the disabled Church. I may say, however, that I have pleaded and now plead for her before the king, who protests that his whole heart is in her preservation, and that any harm done by his officers to our tenants has been done against his will. He says too, and with tears in his eyes regrets, that the importunity of his soldiers has forced him to lay burdens on the Church. Nor is it his Majesty's intention to compel our weary priests to give up the care of souls. His excuse for exacting tribute from the churches to aid the kingdom is that he undertook the war as much for the freedom of the Church as for the safety of the kingdom. I give you this excuse for whatever it is worth. His Majesty promises that when he has paid the enormous debt contracted to Lubeck, and has wholly freed the kingdom, both clergy and people shall rejoice as never they have rejoiced before. In the extirpation of Lutheranism I am aided as much by the efforts of his Majesty as by the authority of the pope. It seems to me that the strife going on by letters among the clergy should be put to an end, and more toleration shown. I know it will, if continued, spread conflagration in other lands. The clergy of Strengnäs have promised me firmly that they will abstain from all new doctrines, and will send out no more letters unless they are harassed." This warning from the legate proves that the Swedish prelates were already cutting one another's throats. Apparently, too, it worked like magic in quieting their disputes, for six months now elapsed before the charge of heresy was raised again.

On the 21st of February, 1524, Laurentius Andreæ returned to the assault with a long epistle to the Vadstena Chapter. This epistle is moderate in tone, and contains this sound advice: "His Majesty desires that when you discover strange doctrines in the books of Luther or of any other, you should not reject them without a fair examination. If then you find anything contrary to the truth, write a refutation of it based on Holy Writ. As soon as scholars have seen your answer and have determined what to accept and what reject, you can preach according to their judgment and not according to your individual caprice. I suspect, however, there will hardly be many among you able to refute these doctrines; for, though but little of the so-called Lutheran teaching has come to my knowledge, I am convinced that Luther is too great a man to be refuted by simple men like us, for the Scriptures get their strength from no man, but from God. Even if we have the truth on our side, 'tis folly for us who have no arms to attack those who are well equipped, since we should thus do nothing but expose our own simplicity.... Prove all things; hold fast that which is good. Search the spirit to see whether it be of God. I would urge every one to read the new doctrines. Those who persuade or command you otherwise, appear to me to act contrary to the Scriptures, and I suspect they do not wish the truth to come to light.... If there be any among you whom this letter offends, let him write to me, pointing out where I am wrong, and I will withdraw my statements." Brask, though offended deeply, scorned the challenge. Instead of answering Andreæ, he wrote to the bishop of Skara, saying: "Certain persons are beginning to urge that we should not banish Luther's writings, but should study them carefully to the end that we may write against them, as if, forsooth, we were simple enough to trouble ourselves about the effrontery of Luther. He flatters himself that he possesses greater wisdom than all the saints. But we shall bow the knee to God, not man, and shall do our utmost that the kingdom be not corrupted by this new heresy." Brask was now boiling with indignation, and a few days later wrote a friend: "I have no fear of Luther or any other heretic. Were an angel from heaven to predict his victory, I should not waver."

This feigned assurance on the part of Brask was not deep-set. In the secrecy of his own cloisters he contemplated the issue with fear and trembling. This is clear from a letter penned at this period to the monarch. "By the allegiance which I owe you," wrote the bishop, "I deem it my duty to urge you not to allow the sale of Luther's books within the realm, nor give his pupils shelter or encouragement of any kind, till the coming council of the Church shall pass its judgment.... I know not how your Grace can better win the love of God, as well as of all Christian kings and princes, than by restoring the Church of Christ to the state of harmony that it has enjoyed in ages past." The same day that this letter was despatched, Brask wrote to a friend in terms which show that his anxiety was great. After intimating that the king's constant demands on him for money were probably inspired by the friends of Luther, he exclaimed: "This party is growing all too fast among us, and I greatly fear lest some new heresy, which God forbid! may break out soon." As the king appeared not likely to take very stringent measures to repress the heresy, the bishop hastened to exert his own authority, and issued a mandate, to be read from all the pulpits in his diocese, forbidding the sale of Luther's books and teachings. A few days later the monarch's answer came. It was couched in temperate language, but offered little solace to the bishop. "Regarding your request," so wrote Gustav, "that we forbid the sale of Luther's writings, we know not by what right it could be done, for we are told his teachings have not yet been found by impartial judges to be false. Moreover, since writings opposed to Luther have been circulated through the land, it seems but right that his, too, should be kept public, that you and other scholars may detect their fallacies and show them to the people. Then the books of Luther may be condemned. As to your charge that Luther's pupils are given shelter at our court, we answer that they have not sought it. If indeed they should, you are aware it is our duty to protect them as well as you. If there be any in our protection whom you wish to charge, bring your accusation and give their names." The method of trial suggested in this letter was not in harmony with the bishop's views. What he wanted was an inquisition, and inwriting to a fellow-bishop he did not hesitate to say so. "I maintain that every diocese should have an inquisition for this heresy, and I think our Most Holy Father ought to write his Majesty to that effect." The mere prohibition of Luther's writings was of no avail. As Brask declared to Johannes Magni, "The number of foreign abettors of Lutheranism is growing daily, despite our mandate, through the sale of Luther's books. I fear the remedy will be too late unless it is applied at once."

This letter was written on the 20th of June, 1524. About the same time Petri was called to Stockholm to fill the post of city clerk, and Andreæ, already secretary to the king, was made archdeacon of Upsala. This double advancement of the Lutheran leaders left no room longer to doubt the king's designs. From this time forth he was felt on every hand to be an enemy to the Romish Church. The striking fact in all this history is the utter absence of conscientious motives in the king. Though the whole of Christendom was ablaze with theological dispute, he went on steadily reducing the bishops' power with never a word of invective against their teaching or their faith. His conduct was guided solely by a desire to aggrandize the crown, and he seized without a scruple the tools best fitted to his hand. Had Brask been more compliant, or the Church less rich, the king would not unlikely have continued in the faith. The moral of all this is to hide your riches from those that may become your foes.

The part that Brask played in this drama calls forth a feeling of respect. Artful and manœuvring though he was, there were certain deep principles within his breast that only great adversity could touch. Of these the most exalted was his affection for the Church. Apart from all her splendor and the temporal advantages to which her service led, Brask loved her for herself. She was the mother at whose breast he had been reared, and the feelings that had warmed his soul in childhood could not easily be extinguished now that he was old. Every dart that struck her pierced deep into his own flesh, and a premonition of the coming ruin overwhelmed him with bitter grief. It was this very grief, however, that raised him to rebel. The old vacillating temper that he had shown in days gone by was his no longer. Drear and dismal though the prospect was, he did not hesitate, but threw himself into the encounter heart and soul. From this time forth, with all his cunning and sagacity, he was the steadfast leader of the papal cause.

RELIGIOUS DISCORD AND CIVIL WAR. 1524-1525.

BY the autumn of 1524 the whole of Sweden was in a ferment of theological dispute. When Gustav returned from the congress of Malmö to the capital, he found the people in a wild frenzy of religious zeal. The turmoil was occasioned mainly by the efforts of two Dutchmen, Melchior and Knipperdolling, who had renounced their respective callings as furrier and huckster to spread abroad the teachings of a new religious sect. The history of this strange movement has been so often told that it is hardly necessary to waste much time upon it here. It originated doubtless in the stimulus that Luther's preaching had given to religious thought. As so frequently occurs, the very enthusiasm which the Reformers felt for things divine led them to disregard their reason and give their passions undivided sway. One of the chronicles puts it: "Wherever the Almighty builds a church, the Devil comes and builds a chapel by its side." The thing that most distinguished these weird Dutchmen was their communistic views. They taught that, since we all were equal in the eyes of God, we should all be equal likewise in the eyes of men, that temporal government along with class distinctions of every kind should be abolished, and that Christians should indulge in absolute community of goods. In religious matters, too, they had peculiar views, believing that only adults should receive baptism, and that all adults who had been baptized in infancy should be baptized again. By reason of this tenet they were known as Anabaptists. Their first appearance in the Swedish capital occurred at a moment when the monarch was away. In that, at any rate, they manifested sense. The capital was all agog with Luther's doctrines, and everything that bore the stamp of novelty was listened to with joy. Melchior and Knipperdolling were received with open arms, the pulpits were placed at their disposal, and men and women flocked in swarms to hear them. The town authorities raised no opposition, believing the influence of these teachers would be good. In a short time, however, they were undeceived. The contagion spread like wildfire through the town, and every other citizen began to preach. Churches, monasteries, and chapels were filled from morn till eve, and pulpits resounded with doctrines of the most inflammatory kind. All government was set at naught, and every effort to stay the tempest merely added to its force. Finally these fanatics made war upon the altars, throwing down statues and pictures, and piling the fragments in huge heaps about the town. They dashed about like maniacs, a witness writes, not knowing what they did. How far their madness would have led them, it is idle to conceive. Gustav returned to Stockholm while the delirium was at fever heat, and his presence in an instant checked its course. He called the leaders of the riot before him, and demanded sharply if this raving lunacy seemed to them religion. They mumbled some incoherent answer, and, the fury having spent its force, most of them were reprimanded and discharged. Melchior with one or two others was kept in jail awhile, and then sent back to Holland, with orders not to return to Sweden on pain of death. Some ten years later Melchior was executed along with Knipperdolling for sharing in the famous riot of the Anabaptist sect in Münster.

The hurricane had swept past Stockholm and was gone, but evils of every kind existed to attest its force. Among the greatest sufferers from this fanaticism were the partisans of Luther. Their attitude to the rioters had at first been doubtful, and the condemnation heaped on Melchior and Knipperdolling fell partially on them. People in general could not distinguish between fanatics and Luther. They were all deemed heretics, and Gustav was roundly cursed for neglecting the religion of his fathers. To soothe the people Gustav planned a journey through the realm, intending to set forth before the autumn closed. This journey he was forced by stress of circumstances to postpone. He therefore turned to other methods to effect his end. The strongest feature of the Lutheran doctrine was that it purported to be based upon the Word of God. To such a pretension no one but an unbeliever could object. Lutheranism was opposed on the ground of its presumed basis in the idiosyncrasies of men. Gustav, confident that this idea was false, resolved to put the question to a test. Accordingly, among matters to be discussed at the Cabinet meeting in October, we find a proposition that all priests be ordered to confine their teaching to the Word of God. The fate of this sound measure is not known. It appears nowhere in the list of subjects on which the Cabinet took a vote. A fair conclusion is that the question was too broad to be determined at the time, and therefore was omitted from the calendar by consent of all.

Gustav was determined, however, that the matter should not drop. Convinced that any discord inside the Church would be a benefit to the crown, he resolved to hold a theological disputation, and selected a champion from the two chief factions, with orders to appear at Christmas in Upsala and defend the doctrines of his party in open court. The Lutheran gladiator of course was Petri, his opponent being one Peder Galle, a learned canon of Upsala. The main points that were discussed are these: man's justification; free will; forgiveness of sins; invocation and worship of saints; purgatory; celebration of vigils and masses for the dead; chanting of the service; good works, and rewards; papal and monastic indulgences; sacraments; predestination; excommunication; pilgrimages. The battle on these questions was fought, December 27, in the Chapter-house at Upsala; and the chronicle tells us, somewhat unnecessarily, that the fight was hot. Each party was struggling for the very kernel of his faith. If the Bible were acknowledged to be our sole authority in religious things, the whole fabric of the papal Church was wrong. On the other hand, if power were granted to the Fathers to establish doctrines and methods supplementary to the Bible, the Lutherans had no right to disobey. As Gustav was arbiter of the battle, there could be no doubt of the result. Petri is asserted to have come off victor, on the ground that his citations were all from Holy Writ.

Flattered by this great victory, the Lutherans grew bold. Though not so turbulent as before the riot, they showed much indiscretion, and Gustav often found it necessary to interfere. What annoyed him chiefly was their bravado in alluding to the popes and bishops. The hierarchy of Romanism was fixed so firmly in people's hearts that every effort to dislodge it caused a jar. Especially in the rural districts was it necessary not to give alarm. A single deed or word might work an injury which many months of argument could not efface. It is not strange, therefore, that the king was troubled when Petri, in February, 1525, violated every rule of Church propriety by being married publicly in Stockholm. The marriage fell like a thunderclap upon the Church. Brask apparently could not believe his ears. He dashed off a letter to another prelate to inquire whether the report was true, and finding that it was, wrote to the archbishop as well as to the king, denouncing the whole affair. "Though the ceremony has been performed," he argued, "the marriage is invalid, for such was the decree made by the sixth Council of the Church." In his letter to the king, Brask used these words: "Your Majesty must be aware that much talk has been occasioned by the marriage in your capital of Olaus Petri, a Christian priest. At a future day, should the marriage result in children, there will be much trouble, for the law declares that children of a priest shall stand, in matters of inheritance, on a par with bastards.... Even in the Grecian Church, where persons who are married may be ordained on certain terms, those already priests have never been allowed to marry. Petri's ceremony is not a lawful marriage, and places him under the ban, according to the doctrines of the Church. For God's sake, therefore, act in this matter as a Christian prince should do." On receiving this letter, Gustav, who had been in Upsala when the act occurred, called for the offending preacher and asked him what excuse he offered for violating the ancient customs of the Church. To this the culprit answered that he was ready to defend his conduct in open court, and prove that the laws of God should not be sacrificed to the laws of men. The king then wrote to Brask and assured him that if Petri should be shown to have done wrong, he should be punished. The king's own prejudices are manifest in the words with which his letter closed. "As to your assertion," he said, "that Petri's act has placed him under the ban, it would seem surprising if that should be the effect of marriage,—a ceremony that God does not forbid,—and yet that for debauchery and other sins which are forbidden, one should not fall beneath the ban.... In making this charge concerning Petri, you appear elated at the opportunity thus given you to censure me." This last insinuation the bishop strenuously denied. "God knows," he wrote the king, "that I have acted for your welfare in this matter, as well as for my own. What joy I or any other could feel in my present age and infirmity, I leave to God. Petri has sent me an apology for his act. It is full of words, but void of sense. I shall see to it, however, that it gets an answer."

These stormy scenes within the Church were but the echo of what was going on outside. As the autumn advanced it became each day more clear that Fredrik had victimized the king at Malmö. The Swedish army had retired from Gotland, and Norby with his horde of pirates remained *in statu quo*. Brask, who had the interests of Sweden constantly at heart, was the first person to suspect foul play. So early as December 9 he told a friend his fears had been aroused. Gustav, if he had suspicions, kept them dark. He opened correspondence with Norby, hoping to inveigle him into a conference in Stockholm. Norby, however, knew the trick himself. The weather was such, he answered, that he could not come. Some few weeks later Gustav wrote to Mehlen that the promises made to him at Malmö had not been fulfilled. He also sent his messengers to Denmark denouncing Norby's course. But all this time his communications with Norby were filled with warm assurance of respect.

The truth was, Norby cherished a project far more ambitious than either Fredrik or Gustav could suppose. In January, 1524, the brave Christina, widow of the young Sten Sture, had returned to Sweden after her long captivity in Denmark. The same ambitious spirit that had filled her breast in earlier days was with her still, and she longed to see upon her son's head the crown that but for his early death would have been worn by her husband. This son, a mere boy of twelve, had recently returned from Dantzic, whither he had been sent as exile four years before by Christiern. He had disembarked at Kalmar, and still remained there under custody of Mehlen. In this state of affairs the piratical Norby conceived the project of marrying Christina, and then of conjuring with the name of Sture to drive Gustav out of Sweden. To this bold scheme Christina apparently gave her consent. At all events, the news of her projected marriage was spread abroad, and nothing was done on her part to deny it.

Norby's chief anxiety was to get possession of the boy. Mehlen had shown reluctance to give him to Christina, and one might readily conclude his purpose was to hand him over to the king. Such a purpose, however, Mehlen seems never to have entertained. He preferred to watch developments, and at the proper moment resign his charge to the party that should make the highest bid. The truth is, Mehlen had fallen into disrepute. His pusillanimous conduct in the siege of Visby had gradually dawned upon the king, and ere the close of 1524 report was spread that Mehlen had incurred his monarch's wrath. Though summoned to Stockholm in January to the marriage of the monarch's sister, he did not venture to appear, but wrote a letter to Gustav begging for a continuance of favor at the court. The answer that came back was characteristic of the king. Stripped of all its verbiage, it was an assurance that the general report was wrong. Mehlen might still bask in the smiles of royalty, and must pay no heed to public slander. In confirmation of these sentiments Gustav induced the Cabinet to enclose a letter. "Dear brother," the Cabinet lovingly began, "we hear a rumor is abroad that you have grown distasteful to the king, and you are said to shun his presence in fear of danger to your life. We declare before Almighty God we never heard the monarch speak one word in your disfavor, though we can well believe there may be slanderers who would rejoice to see such discord spread. We doubt not you will stamp out such discord with your utmost power. Therefore we beg you pay no heed to evil messengers, but come here at the earliest opportunity to the king." This urgent exhortation meeting with no response, some three weeks later the monarch wrote again, still with a show of friendship, but insisting on the immediate presence of the erstwhile favorite in Stockholm. So imperative an order Mehlen dared not disobey. Proceeding at once to Stockholm, he appeared before the king, and soon discovered that his worst suspicions were not far from true. The assurances of his monarch's favor had been a blind to decoy the officer away from Kalmar. On the 12th of March Gustav removed him from the post, and appointed another officer, Nils Eriksson, in his stead. Anticipating that the change might cause some friction, the monarch sent off a whole batch of letters in explanation of his act. One of these letters, though a trifle lengthy, is perhaps worth quoting. It is addressed to the fief of Kalmar, and runs in this wise: "Dear friends, we thank you warmly for the devotion and allegiance which you, as true and loyal subjects, have exhibited toward us as well as toward the kingdom of your fathers. You will remember that last summer, when we despatched our fleet to Gotland to besiege Norby in the castle and town of Visby, and when he found that he could expect no aid from Christiern, he sent his ambassadors to take oath of allegiance to Fredrik, King of Denmark. His purpose, which we clearly saw, was simply to cause dissension between the kingdoms, thus giving Christiern opportunity to come forward and seize the reins once more. It appearing to us and to our Cabinet unwise to permit a new war at that time to spring up between the kingdoms, we proceeded with delegates from our Cabinet to a congress of the realms at Malmö. There we made a permanent alliance with each other and the Hanseatic Towns against King Christiern. We agreed, moreover, that our respective claims to Gotland should be left to arbitration. When, now, Norby saw that the dissension which he had longed for was not likely to ensue, he disregarded every oath that he had made to Fredrik, and continued in his old allegiance to King Christiern. He also feigned a willingness to come to terms with us, if we would protect his interests in this kingdom. This he offered, as we have now found out, in hope of causing discord between us and the Hanseatic Towns. He has, too, spread a rumor among the Danes and Germans that we had entered into an alliance with him against them. Of any such alliance we assure you we are ignorant. Now, as to Mehlen, we are told he does not wholly please you. We have therefore recalled him from his post, and made Nils Eriksson commander of Kalmar Castle and governor of the town and fief. We beg you be submissive and pay to him all rents and taxes which fall due until we find an opportunity to visit you in person. He will govern you, by God's help, according to Saint Erik's law and the good old customs of your fathers. If any among you are found encouraging dissension or engaged in plots, we pray you all be zealous in aiding Eriksson to bring them to destruction." Along with this letter Gustav sent one to the burghers in the town of Kalmar. It appears they had protested against the taxes imposed on them by Mehlen. There can be little doubt these taxes were imposed by order of the king. As matters stood, however, it seemed poor policy to claim them. These are the monarch's words: "Some of your fellow-townsmen have let us understand that taxes have been laid on you for which you are in no wise liable. We have already written you that you are to be free therefrom; but that letter, we now are told, has never reached you. God knows we grieve extremely that any such burden should have been imposed against our wish and orders, and we hereby notify you that we shall not claim these taxes laid on you by Mehlen." Simultaneously with this document others of like tenor were despatched to other persons to allay their wrath.

These summary proceedings of Gustav made Mehlen more ready to accept proposals from the other side; and he was further impelled in that direction by recent plots among the Dalesmen. The insurrection under Sunnanväder, which the monarch had fancied he could extinguish by a generous supply of salt, had not yet yielded to the treatment. Indeed, according to the best reports, the malady had spread. How serious the insurrection was, appears from the frequency of the monarch's exhortations. All through the winter he was writing to the people, condoling with them for the exorbitant price of food, and attributing all their evils to the continuance of wars in Europe. The Cabinet also addressed the Dalesmen, urging them not to ally themselves with Sunnanväder, who was disgruntled, so they heard, because he had not been given the bishopric of Vesterås. In one of his appeals Gustav warned the rebels to be still, lest Christiern might be encouraged to return. The spectre of their gory tyrant seems not, however, to have haunted them, and in February we find that Knut, the deposed dean of Vesterås, had joined their ranks. To him Gustav wrote a note, assuring him that the archbishopric would have been conferred upon him had he but done his duty. Knut, apparently, did no great benefit to his brother's cause. Only a few days after he arrived, his leader wrote archly to a person who had loaned him funds, that he could stay no longer in the land, for certain peasants were already on his track, intending to capture him and take him to the king. If these suspicions were correct, it was probably as well for him that he escaped. Some two weeks later these two scoundrels were both in Norway, waiting for a more auspicious moment to return.

Whether their movements were in any way inspired by Norby, is not clear. One thing, however, is very sure. Whomever Norby thought could be of service, he did not hesitate to use. In the previous summer, even while truckling with Fredrik, he had been in steady communication with Christiern, who was Fredrik's bitter foe. And now, though every one believed him to have broken with Fredrik, there was a story afloat that Fredrik's hand was really behind the pirate's opposition to Gustav. No one could place the slightest confidence in what he said. In January he started a rumor that he was ready to give up Gotland, provided the king would grant him a like domain in Finland; but soon it turned out that the whole project was a ruse. In February he had so far befogged the intellect of Fredrik as to induce that monarch to request of Gustav a full pardon for all of Norby's doings. It need scarce be added, this ridiculous proposal met with no success; and Fredrik, almost as soon as it was sent, had cause to rue it, for Norby toward the close of winter sent an army into Bleking,—a province ceded to Fredrik by the Congress of Malmö,—and there spread ruin far and wide.

The relations of Fredrik to Sweden at this juncture are very strange. Though nominally at peace, the two nations were utterly distrustful of each other, and at frequent intervals tried in secret to cut each other's throats. Their only bond of union was their common abhorrence of the tyrant Christiern; and whenever Fredrik fancied that danger averted, he spared no effort to humiliate his rival beyond the strait. One instance of his treachery was noticed in the comfort given to Knut and Sunnanväder when they fled to Norway. The treaty of Malmö had stated with sufficient clearness that all fugitives from one country to the other should be returned; and Fredrik, as king of Norway, was bound to see to it that the treaty was observed. It cannot be stated positively that he encouraged the fugitives himself, but it is very certain that his officers in Norway did, and that he made no effort to restrain them.

The share Christina had in this conspiracy is likewise doubtful. So early as February Gustav suspected her, and ordered one of his officers to keep spies upon her track. As a result one of her servants was detected in treacherous proceedings and arrested. It appears, however, that she did not merit all the king's severity; for Brask in April wrote a friend, that the monarch was treating her with undue harshness. She was widely popular, and Gustav would have been more wise had his hostility to her been less open. "Nescit regnare qui nescit dissimulare," wrote the wily bishop. Christina was not, at any rate, on the best of terms with Mehlen, for her boy was kept in Kalmar till the castle passed from Mehlen's hands.

This last result was not effected till a long time after Mehlen had been deposed. Before leaving Kalmar he had intrusted matters to his brother, with orders not to yield the castle to any but himself. As soon, therefore, as the new officer approached to take his fief, the reply was given him that the castle would not be yielded till Mehlen should return.

After some three weeks spent in futile negotiation, Gustav wrung from Mehlen a letter directed to his brother, instructing him to yield. This the monarch sent to Kalmar, April 8, along with a letter of his own. Convinced that the whole delay on the part of Mehlen was to use up time, he instructed his messenger to warn the occupants that if the castle were not surrendered by the 1st of May, he would make them smart for it. In his letter, however, Gustav used more gentle language. "We have kept your brother here," he wrote, "in order to protect him from the populace, whose mouths are full of scandal about our relations to him. From your letter it appears you thought we held him in confinement.... We are minded to treat him well and kindly, unless we shall be forced by you to treat him otherwise. We warn you, however, we shall deal with Kalmar in the way that we deem best, for the town and castle belong to God, to us, and to the Swedish crown.... Our counsel is that you obey our mandate, and the earlier you do so the better it will be for you." Accompanying this letter was a passport, similar to one drawn up for Mehlen, to take his brother from the realm. He was not, however, to be allured by passports or even terrified by threats. The castle continued firm, and Gustav began to levy forces to besiege it.

While these forces were being gathered, Gustav renewed his efforts to gain favor through the land. This he soon discovered to be no easy task. Surrounded by conspirators on every hand, he could not turn without confronting some new rumor. Stories of the most contradictory nature were set afloat each day. At one time the report was spread through Dalarne that he had cast Christina into jail. After that it was rumored that he was sending despatches frequently to Gotland, from which some persons caught the notion he was in secret league with Norby. This notion was so baleful that Gustav felt it best to answer it. "No one need think," he said, "we attach the slightest importance to anything that Norby says. As he asked us for a hearing, we have promised to let him have it. He used smooth words to us, and we have given him smooth answers in return.... As to these slanderous stories," continued Gustav, in writing to an officer, "you are aware we cannot close men's mouths. We believe our actions toward our people will bear examination before both God and man." Such an examination he proposed to make, and on the 25th of March he sent out notice of a general diet to be held in the early part of May. This notice contained among other things these startling words: "If it shall happen that the Cabinet and people then assembled believe the present evils are in any respect the outcome of our methods of government, we shall lay it before them to determine whether they wish us to continue in the government or not. It was at their request and exhortation that we assumed the reins at Strengnäs, and whatever their judgment now may be, it shall be followed." In addition to this notice, sent to all portions of the land, Gustav wrote to the people of Mora that he had heard of a complaint from them that the kingdom was going to pieces and that he was causing it. He assured them that the rumor was untrue, and that he was doing all he could to hold the realm together. When these assurances reached Dalarne, the poor peasants of that district were already starving. Half mad with hunger, they called a mass meeting of their little parishes, and drew up a heart-rending though unfair statement of their wrongs. A copy of these grievances they despatched at once to Stockholm. It charged the king with appointing German and Danish officers to the highest positions in the state, and with quartering foreign soldiers in the towns and villages till the inhabitants were constrained to flee. He had further, they asserted, laid taxes on the monasteries and churches, and on the priests and monks; he had seized jewels consecrated to God's service; he had robbed the churches of all their Swedish money, and substituted "klippings," which he then had repudiated; and he had seized the tithes. Finally they charged him with imprisoning Christina and her boy. The letter ended with a warning that unless he at once drove out all foreigners, released Christina with the others whom he had in prison, and took some measures to better trade, they would renounce allegiance to him. Gustav received this document while the diet was in session. His answer to the people of Dalarne contained these words: "We cannot believe this letter was issued by your consent. Rather, we think, it was inspired by certain wiseacres among you hoodwinked by Sunnanväder and the like. That the purpose of these men is to bring back Christiern we have definite proofs, not only within the kingdom but without. Ever since Sunnanväder went among you, letters and messengers have been passing between Dalarne and Norby, the meaning of all which is that Norby is to attack the government on one side and Dalarne on the other, and that we are to be dragged down from the throne, which is then to be handed over to Norby for the benefit of Christiern." This letter reflected in some degree the spirit of the diet. The main object for which it had been called was to spread an impression that the king was acting as representative of his people. It was not asked to legislate, and it did not do so. Gustav, however, went through the farce which he had promised, and asked the delegates if they wished him to resign the crown. Of course the answer was a shower of plaudits upon the king. As Gustav modestly puts it, "The Cabinet and people over all the land besought us not to resign, but govern them hereafter as heretofore; and they promised obedience as in the past, swearing by hand and mouth to risk in our service their lives and everything they had." With this seductive ceremony the diet was dismissed.

Ere the diet had come together, Norby had made a second irruption into Fredrik's territory in the south of Sweden. Toward the end of March he had sailed from Gotland with twelve men-of-war, had captured a couple of the strongest fortresses in Bleking, and had enlisted many inhabitants of that province in the cause of Christiern. Fredrik was by this time fully alive to the error he had made in relying for a moment on the promises of Norby. His anxiety was increased still further when the news was brought him that Christiern's brother-in-law, the emperor, had defeated the king of France, and was coming with all his forces to the relief of Christiern. One drop of comfort was granted him when he heard that a fleet from Lubeck had sailed to Gotland in Norby's absence, and on May 13 had seized the town of Visby. In spite of this disaster, Norby's hopes ran high. He sent letters every day to Christiern, telling him that Denmark as well as Sweden was overrun with rebels, and that he now had a chance of restoration such as he had never had before. But Norby's hopes were at the very highest when the bubble burst. The emperor proved too busy with his own affairs to send his army to the North, and Christiern could not raise the armament requisite for a foreign war. Gustav, moreover, sent his troops to drive back the invader, and the Danish nobility enlisted in behalf of Fredrik. The result was that ere the close of May the pirate was routed in two important battles. Gustav literally hugged himself for joy, and sent off a letter of congratulation to the army that had won the day. "My good men," he began, "you may rest assured that if Norby shall escape you and come this way, he will meet with a reception that will cause him little joy. From his assertion that he expected aid from us, you will perceive he sought to foster discord between your realm and us.... We had already ordered our men in Vestergötland to go to your relief as soon as you should need them, which now, thank God, we trust will never be." The monarch's congratulation was a little premature. Norby's force was scattered, but it was not lost. Retiring with his stragglers to one of the Danish strongholds, he ensconced himself within, and there remained,—a constant menace to the neighborhood. Late in June the pirate, reduced to the utmost extremity, opened negotiations with Fredrik. That monarch, still in dread of Christiern, readily complied. Norby proceeded to Copenhagen, where it was finally arranged that he should yield the castle of Visby, which the Lubeck army had been besieging ever since the town of Visby fell; and that in return the pirate should be granted the whole province of Bleking with all its strongholds, to hold as a fief of Denmark. Norby was then conveyed to Denmark, and before the first of August these terms were carried out. Visby passed into the hands of Lubeck, and the pirate returned to Bleking to guard his fief.

Gustav, it need scarce be said, was vexed. The congress which was to have been held in Lubeck to discuss his claim to Gotland had been indefinitely postponed. In place thereof, the island had been seized by Lubeck, and Bleking—another of the disputed territories—had been conferred upon a bitter foe. What most irritated him was the close proximity of Norby's fief to Sweden. He was at a loss, moreover, to understand the king of Denmark's motives. "It may be," he suggested in a letter of July 9, "that Fredrik's purpose was to secure Gotland, and then deal with Norby as he pleased. However this may be, we must keep watch on every side." The same day he wrote to another person, "We are in no wise pleased to have Norby for a neighbor, since we have noticed that he always seeks to do us harm." Still, Gustav believed in making a virtue of necessity, and a few days later wrote: "We are glad that hostilities between Fredrik and Norby are at an end, and that the kingdom is once more on the road to peace and quiet."

This letter was written by Gustav in his camp at Kalmar. The castle there was still in the hands of Mehlen's brother, though it had been under siege about two months. Early in June Gustav, unwilling to shed more blood, had ordered Mehlen to proceed to Kalmar and bid the castle yield. The confidence with which the monarch even yet regarded Mehlen is astounding, and the issue proved at once the monarch's folly. On reaching Kalmar, Mehlen, after a conference with Eriksson, was allowed to enter the castle to persuade his men to yield. The following day, the portcullis was lowered and Mehlen came out upon the bridge. But while he pretended to be crossing, a portion of the garrison dashed out of the castle and massacred a number of the people, all unsuspecting, in the town. The alarm was then given to the royal guard, and Mehlen's soldiers, finding themselves outnumbered, retired across the bridge. Five days later, Mehlen, with his wife and brother, scaled the castle wall and sailed for Germany, leaving his wretched soldiers to withstand the siege. If ever there was a cowardly, bustling, impotent, insignificant adventurer, Berent von Mehlen was that man. During his two years' stay in Sweden he had dabbled in every project that arose, and he had accomplished absolutely nothing. He had been the hero of a six months' bloodless siege, that left matters precisely as they had begun; and he had set on foot a conspiracy that had no object and that ended in the air. It is a pleasure to dismiss him from our thoughts. His subsequent career in Germany was of a piece with his career in Sweden. He scurried about from one court to another, endeavoring to raise an army with which to conquer Sweden. But nothing came of any of his projects, and after a short period oblivion settled on his name.

Gustav now learned definitely that Norby, ever since his fleet left Gotland, had been in secret conspiracy with Mehlen. He determined, therefore, that, since the pirate had gained a foothold on the mainland, Kalmar must be secured at any risk. So he collected men from every quarter and sent them down to Kalmar to reinforce the town. Some few weeks later, as the castle had not yielded, he proceeded to the town himself. The burghers, hoping the conflict would now be ended, welcomed him with joy. But the garrison still believed in Mehlen, and confidently awaited his return with aid. Gustav sent an envoy to the castle, to persuade the garrison to yield. The answer was, the garrison would not be yielded till every one of them was dead. But one course, therefore, was open to the monarch,—the castle must be stormed. This, with the guns which he possessed, demanded almost more than human strength. The castle was surrounded on all sides by a moat, beyond which rose a perpendicular wall of masonry twenty feet in height. This rampart was washed on three sides by the sea, and on the other was protected by a broad deep dike and then an outer wall. From within, the rampart was guarded by eight huge towers that stood out from the castle-walls, and the four corners of the ramparts were further strengthened by four more towers with apertures for crossbows, cannon, and muskets. Such was the fortress that Gustav, late in July, resolved to storm. He began by throwing up a line of earthworks, behind which he placed his heavy guns, hoping to batter down the towers and ramparts, while his pikemen and halberdiers were scaling the unprotected parts. But his men at first were lukewarm. The task seemed herculean, and every effort to ascend the ramparts met with certain death. Those in the castle fought like maniacs, the men with guns and crossbows, and the women firing stones. Gustav, it is reported, stormed and swore, and finally put on his armor, declaring that he would either have the castle or die within its walls. His enthusiasm spread among his men, and they shouted they would do their best, though every man of them should fall. The effect was visible at once. Each charge left the ramparts weaker than before; and when night closed in, there was not a tower or rampart whole. The next morning, when Gustav turned his culverins again upon the wall, the flag of truce was raised. The garrison hoped that if they sued before the ramparts actually fell, they might be granted favorable terms. But the monarch, who had now lost nearly half his men, demanded an unconditional surrender. As Norby had been conquered, and no signs of Mehlen's succor had appeared, the garrison, after much palaver, threw themselves upon the mercy of the king. The castle, on the 20th of July, passed into the monarch's hands once more, and a large portion of the rebel garrison was put to death. With this scene the conspiracy of Norby, Mehlen, and their adherents was at an end.

DEALINGS WITH FOREIGN POWERS. 1525-1527.

THE Swedish Revolution was the work of three nations, all foes at heart, endeavoring to effect a common object on utterly divergent grounds. Gustav wished to free his country from a tyrant's rule, while Fredrik's purpose was to gain the throne of Denmark, and Lubeck's was to crush her rival in the Baltic trade. Without the alliance of these three parties, it is not likely that any one of them could have gained his end. So long, therefore, as the common object was in view, each felt an assurance that the others would not fail. It was only when Christiern's power was altogether gone that this triple alliance was dissolved.

The varying hopes of Christiern may be gauged with singular accuracy by Fredrik's show of friendship to Gustav. One cannot read the despatches sent from Denmark without observing a constant change of attitude; the monarch's feelings cooling somewhat as the chance that Christiern would recover Denmark grew more remote. At the moment when Norby returned to Bleking, the movements of Christiern caused the monarch much alarm, and his letters to Gustav were filled with every assurance of good-will. This assurance, however, Gustav took at little more than it was worth. So long as Knut and Sunnanväder were protected by Fredrik's officers in Norway, the Danish monarch's assurances of friendship carried little weight. Gustav seems not to have appealed to Fredrik in this matter till every effort to persuade the Danish officers in Norway had been tried. He wrote even to the Norwegian Cabinet, and begged them to keep the promises made to him in Malmö. While in the midst of these entreaties, a letter came from Fredrik asking for the release of certain prisoners, among them Norby's daughter, whom Gustav had captured in the war with Norby. This was the very opportunity which Gustav craved. He wrote back that in the same war in which these prisoners had been taken, some guns belonging to him had been lost, and he offered to exchange the prisoners for the guns. He requested, further, that Fredrik command his officers in Norway to yield the refugees. While this answer was on the road, Fredrik received a note from Norby, to whom Gustav had written to say that Fredrik had promised that the guns should be returned. Fredrik, therefore, wrote Gustav that these guns were not in his possession, but if the Danish prisoners were surrendered, he would try to get them. When this letter came, the monarch was indignant. Fredrik, it was clear, was playing with him, and hoped to get the prisoners and give nothing in return. The answer which the monarch made was this: "We have just received your letter with excuses for the detention of our guns and ammunition, along with a request for the surrender of Søren Brun, whom you assert we captured in a time of truce. Of such a truce we wish to inform you we are ignorant. He was lawfully taken, inasmuch as he was one of Norby's men.... As to our ammunition you say that it was captured from you and carried off to Gotland. If so, it was no fault of ours. We have written frequently about it, but have met with nothing but delays. If Norby, who you say has sworn allegiance to you, holds this ammunition in Visby Castle, it is unquestionably in your power to order that it be returned. So soon as this is done, the prisoners shall be released." Before this determined letter arrived in Denmark, Fredrik had modified his plans, for news had come that Christiern's fleet was on the way to Norway, intending to winter there and make an incursion into Denmark in the spring. Fredrik, therefore, despatched a note to Norby telling him to yield the ammunition, and wrote Gustav that the guns were ready, and if he would send his officers to Denmark for them they should be delivered. A few days later an officer of Fredrik wrote Gustav that property of Danish subjects had been seized in Sweden, and begged that the persons wronged be recompensed. To this Gustav answered that Swedish subjects had been treated in the same way in Denmark, and promised to observe the treaty if the Danes would do so in return. He likewise wrote to Fredrik thanking him for his action relating to the guns, declaring that he would send for them as requested, and as soon as they were yielded would set the prisoners free.

This amicable adjustment of their difficulty was on paper, but much more shuffling was required before it was reduced to fact. Gustav feared that Fredrik was in league with Norby, and rumor had it that Norby was preparing for another war. Late in 1525, the pirate wrote the Swedish officer in Kalmar that he had come to terms with Fredrik, and that all the injury which he had done to Sweden had been forgiven. To this the officer replied: "I fail to see how Fredrik can have promised that you may keep our ammunition." Norby at all events did keep it, and early in 1526 Gustav wrote: "We hear that Norby has let fall calumnies against us. We place no confidence whatever in him, especially as he is growing stronger every day.... From his own letters we discover he has no thought of giving up our ammunition." To Fredrik himself the monarch wrote: "From Norby's letters we learn he has no intention of obeying your commands." In the same strain Gustav addressed the Danish Cabinet, and expressed the hope that Norby was not acting under their behest. If the Cabinet's assertion can be trusted, he was not; for several of the Cabinet wrote Gustav to keep an eye on Norby, as he was raising a large force in Bleking despite their orders to him to desist. There being little hope that Fredrik would force the pirate to obey, Gustav ventured to arrange the matter for himself. It so happened at this moment that one of Norby's vessels, laden with arms and ammunition, stranded on the coast not far from Kalmar. The monarch's officers hurried to the spot, and seized what ammunition they could find. This stroke, however, was in some degree offset by a reprisal which Norby managed to secure upon the coast of Bleking. Matters now appeared so serious that the king addressed himself to Norby. "We find," he said, "that a part of the ammunition taken from the wreck off Kalmar is our own. All the rest of it you may have, provided we are given the guns and ammunition promised us by Fredrik.... As soon as these are handed over, your daughter and the other prisoners shall be freed." This proposition would have satisfied any man but Norby. To him it seemed unfair. The fleet of Christiern was looked for early in the spring, and Norby thought by waiting to obtain more favorable terms. He wrote back, therefore, that, though Fredrik may have told Gustav he should have his guns, he could not have them, for in the treaty recently drawn up between himself and Fredrik, it had been stipulated that all injury done by him to Sweden should be forgotten, and a part of this injury consisted in the seizure of these guns. Norby closed his letter with an offer to hold a personal conference with the king. The reply which Norby had to this proposal was sharp and warm. "We shall permit no nonsense," wrote the king. If Norby wanted his daughter, let him return the guns. "As to a personal meeting with you, we cannot spare the time." Norby's pride apparently was not touched by this rebuke. He wrote again, simply repeating what he had said before, and in reply obtained another letter from the king. "We have already told you," wrote Gustav, "that you may have your daughter when we get our guns. We were promised them by the treaty of Malmö, which we desire in every particular to observe. And we will hand over the property belonging to you in the wreck off Kalmar, if you will forward to that town our ammunition together with a promise in writing never from this day forth to wrong us or our men." This letter, dated on the 4th of March, was the last communication that passed between the pirate and the king. Norby had at length discovered that he could not dupe the king, and Gustav deemed it folly to continue parley with one whose only object was to use up time.

Unable to accomplish anything with Norby, it was more than ever important that Gustav should be on terms of amity with Fredrik. For the moment it appeared that Fredrik would be fair. At all events, he had made Gustav a generous promise about the guns, and his Cabinet kept Gustav constantly informed about the acts of Norby. In February, when the lakes were frozen, the monarch sent, as Fredrik had suggested, for his ammunition, and intrusted to the same emissary a letter for the Danish king. This letter was in reply to one from Fredrik, asking for the surrender of a Danish refugee. Gustav could not comply with his request, for the refugee was gone; but he seized again the opportunity to mention Sunnanväder. "We earnestly entreat you," were his words, "to write your Cabinet in Norway no longer to protect this man or any of his party." It was certainly time that something should be done by Fredrik, for at the very moment while Gustav was writing this appeal, the Norwegian Cabinet were issuing a passport for the traitors through their realm; and to a request from Gustav for their surrender, the Cabinet offered the absurd excuse that the fugitives themselves protested they were innocent. "However," it was added, "the fugitives will return if they are given your assurance that they may be tried, as priests, before a spiritual tribunal." In this reply the reason for the detention of the fugitives leaked out. They were high in office in the Church, and the archbishop of Trondhem, with whom they had taken refuge, feared the Lutheran tendencies of the king. Fredrik did not wholly share this fear, and on the 4th of March for the first time addressed the archbishop, commanding him to revoke the passport of the renegades. This letter producing no immediate effect, Gustav waited about six weeks, and then despatched to the Cabinet of Norway a safe-conduct for the renegades to be tried before "a proper tribunal," and, if adjudged not guilty, to return to Norway. The passport was directed to the Cabinet of southern Norway, to whom the monarch used these words: "We marvel much at the language of your northern brothers, and particularly that they are deceived by the treachery of these rascals, which is well known hundreds of miles from here, and might be known in Norway if the people were not blind. I might tell you how they lay a long while in Dalarne, and in the name of the people sent deceitful letters through the land, to stir up hostility against us. But as soon as the people began to leave them, and the Dalesmen announced that these letters were not issued with their consent, they betook themselves to Norway.... If, now, the fugitives will come before a proper tribunal, we cannot and we would not refuse to let them do so. We therefore send a safe-conduct to guard them against all wrong, according to their request. If they do not come, it will be manifest whether they are innocent." The safe-conduct, it may be well to say, ran only to the 10th of August following, and no notice apparently was taken of it till near the expiration of that time.

Gustav now devoted himself to the task of fighting Norby. The pirate had given the king of Denmark a written promise that he would do no injury to Sweden, but it was very soon apparent that this promise was not likely to be kept. By the end of January Norby's acts so far aroused suspicion that Gustav ordered spies to enter Bleking and discover Norby's plans. No very definite information, however, was obtained, probably for the reason that Norby did not know his plans himself. He was waiting for intelligence from Christiern. Late in March Gustav fancied the pirate was preparing to depart for Norway. A few days afterwards, Brask wrote the monarch: "A report is spread that Norby has seized some seven or eight small craft and two large ships. I do not comprehend his purpose. Merchants just arrived from Denmark add that the Germans have handed Gotland over to the Danes, though on the other hand it is declared that Lubeck has sent a strong force of men and ammunition to the isle." The day following the writing of this letter, Gustav despatched a note to Finland, with a warning to beware of Norby, for the news had reached him secretly that the pirate was about to make an incursion into Finland. This was followed, after a week's interval, by another letter announcing that Norby's fleet was lying at anchor, all ready to set sail. The monarch's apprehensions proved to be unfounded. Norby had important business nearer home. Christiern had not wintered in Norway, as some persons had supposed he would, but had continued his efforts to raise a force in Holland. His efforts had been attended with some measure of success, and early in May the Swedish Cabinet had word that Christiern had despatched a force of seven or eight thousand men under Gustaf Trolle to make an attack on Denmark. While this fleet was believed to be under sail, the tortuous Norby wrote to Denmark that he was ready to sacrifice his life for Fredrik, and took the opportunity to charge Gustav with every sort of crime. The expedition of Christiern appears to have miscarried, but it so startled Fredrik that he hastened to rid himself of his doubtful ally, Norby. On pretence of wanting an escort for his daughter, about to sail for Prussia, he asked the pirate to come to Copenhagen. Norby, willing though he was to sacrifice his life for Fredrik, thought he scented bait. He could not go, he said, unless he did so in his own vessel attended by seven hundred of his men, and as an additional guaranty demanded at the outset that his men be paid. This was a little more than Fredrik could digest. His answer was a letter to Gustav, declaring that the pirate was in constant communication with Christiern, and meantime spared no efforts to stir up discord between Gustav and himself. He was now preparing with a fleet and body of seven hundred men to make an incursion into Sweden. Should this occur, Gustav might rely upon the aid of Fredrik. For this generous assurance Gustav in his answer thanked the king, and promised, in return, that if the pirate should make war on Denmark, Fredrik might count on him. Despite these mutual promises of fidelity, neither party relied much on the other. Gustav, in a letter to his Cabinet in Finland, openly declared his discontent with Fredrik. However, a common danger kept the allies together, and early in August Gustav sent a fleet to Kalmar Sound with orders to make an incursion into Bleking on the north, at the same moment that Fredrik's fleet was attacking Norby from the south. For some reason Fredrik did not hear of the Swedish movement till the day was won. On August 24 the Danish and Lubeck fleets were lying off the coast of Bleking, and, thinking that an attack would soon be made by land, bore down upon the fleet of Norby. It was an unequal contest, and the allied fleets were victorious. Seven of Norby's vessels were captured, with four hundred of his men. The conquerors then entered Bleking, and placed the district once more under Danish rule. Norby himself escaped across the Baltic Sea to Russia. There he expected to enlist the grand duke in a war against Gustav. He found, however, that he had mistaken the opinions of his host. The grand duke threw him into prison, where he remained two years. At the end of that time he was set at liberty by request of Charles V., under whose banner he then enlisted. After serving about a year, he was killed outside the walls of Florence, whither he had been sent with the emperor's forces to storm the town. "Such was the end," so runs the chronicle, "of one who in his palmy days had called himself a friend of God and an enemy to every man."

Meantime matters had progressed to some extent with Norway. On the 22d of July, the passport issued for the refugees having nearly expired without intimation that it would be used, Gustav wrote to Fredrik: "Sunnanväder and the other fugitives are still maintained with honor in Norway, and are continually plotting new revolt. They receive especial favor from the archbishop of Trondhem, who is said to have appointed one of them his deacon. We have written frequently about them to the Cabinet of Norway, but the more we write the more honor they receive." This charge was proved by subsequent events to be a trifle hasty. Scarce had the letter been despatched when Knut, who was probably the least guilty of the two conspirators, arrived. He came by order of the archbishop of Trondhem, and along with him came a letter from the archbishop, declaring that, as the king had promised the fugitives they should be tried by prelates of the Church, one of them was surrendered. Sunnanväder would likewise have been handed over but that he was ill. The archbishop closed by urging Gustav to show mercy. It is to be noted that the king had never promised that the tribunal should consist of prelates. What he had said was that they should be tried before a "proper tribunal." Doubtless it was customary that priests should not be tried by laymen, but the practice was not invariably followed, and the language of the passport was enough to throw the conspirators on their guard. In a case of conspiracy against the crown, the Swedish Cabinet would seem to be a proper tribunal, and as a matter of fact it was before the Cabinet that this case was tried. The Cabinet consisted of the archbishop of Upsala, three bishops, and eight laymen. Their decree was, in the first place, that the passport did not protect Knut from trial, and secondly, that he was guilty of conspiracy against the crown. The decree was dated August 9. On that very day the king of Denmark wrote Gustav that he had ordered the archbishop of Trondhem to give no shelter to the traitors, and added: "We are told that you are ready to promise them a trial before yourself and the Swedish Cabinet, after which they shall be permitted to go free." Gustav had never promised that they should go free, and it was preposterous for anybody to expect it. The only object of the trial was to give the traitors an opportunity to prove their innocence, and if they failed to do so, it was only fair that they should suffer. As soon as the decree was signed, Gustav wrote the archbishop of Trondhem that Knut had been found guilty, but that his life should be spared to satisfy the archbishop, at any rate until Gustav could learn what the archbishop proposed to do with the other refugees. A similar letter was sent also by the Cabinet, declaring that "many serious charges were made against Knut, which he was in no way able to disprove." One of the Cabinet members, who had been asked by the archbishop to intercede for Knut, wrote back: "His crime is so enormous and so clearly proved by his own handwriting, that there is no hope for him unless by the grace of God or through your intercession." Even Brask wrote: "He has won the king's ill-favor in many ways, for which he can offer no defence." Against such a pressure of public opinion the archbishop of Trondhem dared no longer stand, and on the 22d of September despatched Sunnanväder to the king, adding, with the mendacity of a child, that he had detained him in Norway only in order that he might not flee. Gustav, with grim humor, thanked him for his solicitude, and begged him now to return all other refugees. Sunnanväder was kept in jail till the 18th of February, 1527. He was then brought before a tribunal consisting of the entire Chapter of Upsala, two bishops, and a number of laymen. The king produced some sixty letters written by the traitor, establishing his conspiracy beyond the shadow of a doubt. He was condemned at once, and executed the same day outside the Upsala walls. Three days later, his accomplice, Knut, was similarly put to death in Stockholm. Thus ended a conspiracy which had cost the monarch infinite annoyance, and which during a period of three years had been a constant menace to the realm.

What most annoyed the king at this time was the importunate demands of Lubeck. Ever since Gotland, in the summer of 1525, had fallen into the hands of Lubeck, Gustav had appreciated the necessity of keeping the Hanseatic town in check. So early as August of that year the monarch wrote Laurentius Andreæ: "You have advised us to cling to Lubeck and place no confidence in the Danes, since they have always played us false. We are not sure, however, that even Lubeck can be trusted, for we have no certainty what she has in mind, especially as she is sheltering in Gotland that outspoken traitor, Mehlen." The Swedish envoys, who had arrived in Lubeck too late to meet the Danes, as had been agreed in Malmö, seem to have reached no terms with Lubeck, and, when they returned to Sweden in September, Gotland was in Lubeck's hands, and Lubeck had announced her purpose of defending Mehlen. Her strongest hold on Sweden lay in the fact that Sweden was still her debtor in a very large amount. Early in 1526 this burden had become so great that the Cabinet passed an act decreeing that two thirds of all the tithes accrued for the year just ended should be surrendered by the Church to meet the nation's debt. The announcement of this levy made Lubeck for the moment more importunate than before. Believing that the money would soon be pouring in, she kept her envoys constantly dogging the monarch's steps, and in the month of April Gustav wrote: "Our creditors will scarce permit us to leave the castle-gate." They were, therefore, as greatly disappointed as Gustav when the money did not come. In June Gustav wrote that he had got together ten thousand marks,—a mere nothing,—and that Lubeck had written to demand immediate payment of the whole. "Her envoys have now closed our doors so tight that it is hardly possible for us to go out." It was clear that some new scheme must be devised, and on the 23d of June the king applied to certain members of his Cabinet. "We have now," he wrote, "as frequently before, had letters from Lubeck demanding in curt language the payment of her debt. You are aware that we have often, especially in Cabinet meetings, asked you to suggest some mode of meeting this requirement, and have never yet been able to elicit any tangible response. Indeed, you have not had the matter much at heart, but have rather left it to be arranged by us. You have, it is true, suggested that the tithes be used, but we find that, though we much relied upon them, they are but a tittle. Our entire taxes for last year, including iron, skins, butter, salmon, amounted to somewhat over ten thousand marks. This sum, which would naturally be used to pay the expenses of our court, has been handed over to pay the debt. The tithes received, which we were assured would be a considerable sum, are shown by our books not to have exceeded two thousand marks in all. The treasury balance has now run so low that we have but a trifle left, and our soldiers, who are now much needed to keep off Christiern and Norby, must be paid. We therefore beg you take this matter seriously to heart, and devise some means by which the debt may soon be paid.... It is utterly impossible from the taxes alone to keep an army and pay this heavy debt, for the taxes are no greater than they were some years ago, though the expenses are very much increased; and, moreover, we have no mines to turn to, as our fathers had." This urgent appeal inspired the Cabinet to act, and at a meeting held in August they provided that a new tax be laid on every subject in the realm. In the table that accompanied this Act, the amounts to be contributed by the different provinces were accurately fixed, as well as the amounts to be collected in the towns. The bishops, too, were called upon to furnish each his quota, based upon an estimate of his means: the archbishop of Upsala paying four thousand marks, the bishop of Åbo three thousand marks, Linköping two thousand five hundred marks, Skara and Strengnäs each two thousand marks, Vesterås one thousand marks, and Vexiö five hundred marks. The amount imposed on Åbo seems unreasonably large, which is probably to be accounted for by the fact that Åbo was not present at the meeting. Brask, in writing to Åbo, told the bishop that his quota was three thousand marks, but did not name to him the individual amounts to be contributed by the other bishops. Gustav, in a letter to the members of his Cabinet in Finland, was even more unfair. He told them that Åbo was to pay three thousand marks, and added that Linköping and Skara were to pay the same. Brask's letter is particularly important in that it puts the balance of the debt to Lubeck at forty-five thousand Lubeck marks, equivalent to ninety thousand Swedish marks, of which amount the archbishop and bishops were expected to raise fifteen thousand marks. Brask, with his usual shrewdness, urged the king to pay the debt that autumn, and thus get rid of Lubeck before the winter came. Gustav doubtless shared with him this view, but there were several grave difficulties in the way. Early in October the monarch held a conference with the Lubeck envoys, and found the balance, as they figured it, to be larger than he had supposed. Moreover, the peasants in the north of Sweden declared they could not spare the funds, and urged Gustav to postpone the levy till a more convenient time. So that at the close of 1526 the Lubeck envoys were still clamoring for their pay.

The cramped position in which Gustav was held by Lubeck made it of great importance that he should be on amicable terms with other powers. So early as 1523, he had sent ambassadors to Russia to ratify the treaty made by Sture. They had returned, however, with announcement that the grand duke's envoys would come to Stockholm and arrange the terms. This promise had never been fulfilled. As soon, therefore, as opportunity was found, the monarch prepared to send ambassadors again. The person to whom the matter was intrusted was the monarch's brother-in-law, Johan von Hoya. In November, 1525, this officer, who had just returned from an expedition to Lubeck, set sail for Finland, where he already had been granted fiefs, with orders to determine whether or not it was desirable that the embassy should go. Considerable delay ensued because Gustav was in want of funds. He thought that since the expedition would be mainly for the benefit of Finland, the cost of sending it should be borne by her. It was, therefore, not till May of 1526, when Russian depredations became unbearable in Finland, that an arrangement could be made. Envoys then were sent to Moscow, and presented to the grand duke a letter from Gustav under date of 20th of May. In this document the monarch stated that his envoys had once before been sent to Moscow to ratify the treaty made with Sture, but for some reason had never reached the capital. Since then great injury had been done in Finland by Russian subjects. Gustav desired, therefore, to renew the treaty, and begged the grand duke to recompense his subjects, and also to make known to him in what towns in Russia his subjects would be allowed to trade. This letter appears to have been some months upon the road, for the grand duke's answer was not given till the 2d of September. In this answer he declared that the previous embassy of Gustav had held a conference with Russian envoys, and by them the treaty made with Sture had been ratified. Swedish merchants were allowed to trade in all the towns of Russia, and all wrongs done to Swedish subjects should be punished and the persons injured recompensed. On the other hand, he should expect Gustav to punish his own subjects for wrongs which they had done in Russia, and all buildings by them erected on Russian soil must be torn down. While the Swedish envoys were returning with this letter, Norby reached the grand duke and complained that Swedes had injured Russian subjects in Lapland. The grand duke therefore ordered that Gustav be notified of the complaint, and asked to punish the offenders if the charge were true. When the embassy returned to Sweden, and the monarch found they had not yet obtained the grand duke's seal, he resolved to go to Finland in the spring of 1527 and meet the Russian emissaries there. This plan, however, was given up for lack of funds, and the Russian emissaries were asked to meet the king in Stockholm. The offer was accepted, the emissaries came, and after an elaborate exchange of costly presents, both parties signed a ratification of the treaty made for seventy years with Sture. The ratification was dated on the 26th of May.

The main reason why Gustav dreaded a rupture between himself and Lubeck was that it would cause great injury to his commerce. Immediately after his election in 1523, the monarch in a moment of enthusiasm had conferred on Lubeck, Dantzic, and their allies a perpetual monopoly of Swedish trade. In an earlier century, when these so-called Vend Cities controlled the Baltic trade, Lubeck would have claimed the monopoly even without a grant. But another branch of the Hanse Towns had ere this grown up in Holland, with a power so formidable that the Vend Cities dared not assert their claim. So long, however, as the privileges granted Lubeck were unrepealed, the Dutch Towns were reluctant to incur her enmity by sending ships to Sweden. The result was that practically all imports came from Lubeck, and when relations between that city and Gustav became a trifle strained, great difficulty was experienced in obtaining food. To remedy this evil, the envoys sent to Lubeck in 1525, finding themselves too late for the congress with the Danes, entered into negotiations with the Dutch envoys that happened to be there. They found at once that Holland wished to trade in Sweden, and was ready to do so if the terms could be arranged. As a provisional measure, the ambassadors on both sides promised, August 17, that the two nations should remain at peace during the next three years, and before the end of that time another congress should be held to make a more systematic treaty. It was agreed further that in the coming autumn a consignment of salt and other wares should be forwarded by the Dutch to Sweden. Apparently this consignment did not come till the spring of 1526, but both parties were eager to arrange a treaty, and it was agreed that a congress for this purpose should be held in Bremen, May 20, 1526. This congress was afterwards postponed, though the Swedish envoy brought a ratification of the former treaty signed by Gustav under date of May 12, 1526, and promised further that salt should be admitted into Sweden free. A similar ratification was signed by Charles V., Sept. 19, 1526. This accomplished, Holland opened negotiations with Sweden to the end that all articles of commerce be placed upon the free-list along with salt; and she requested further that all the Swedish harbors be open to her ships. So ambitious a proposal terrified Gustav. He would have been rejoiced to grant it, but he feared by doing so to irritate Lubeck. It is somewhat amusing to trace the steps by which he convinced himself that such a course was right. Brask, as usual, was the first to question whether Lubeck would consent. On the 9th of December, 1526, he wrote: "I advocate the treaty, but I doubt much whether Lubeck will not raise objections, for she has wished to have the Baltic to herself." A few days later Gustav put out a feeler to his Cabinet in the south of Sweden. "So far as we know," he wrote with caution, "our relations with Lubeck and the Vend Cities do not forbid this treaty." By the spring of 1527 he had grown more confident of his position, and wrote as follows: "The provisional arrangement made with Holland has proved greatly to our advantage. We now desire to make a perpetual treaty with her before Whitsunday next, and for this purpose recommend that Olaus Magni be sent at once to Amsterdam." Two weeks after this he added: "The privileges which the German cities wrung from us in Strengnäs are so grinding that we can no longer adhere to them in all their points." On the 22d of April the monarch had so far removed his doubts as to commission Magni to negotiate the treaty, and he intrusted him with a written promise over the royal signature and seal, conferring on Holland, Brabant, Zealand, and East and West Friesland the right to enter all the Swedish rivers and harbors, on payment of the customary duties. It is noticeable that in this document Gustav did not remit the duties, as had been desired, nor even promise that salt should be admitted free; and in the letter to his envoy the diplomatic monarch used these words: "Do not be too liberal, especially in the matter of duties. If they really insist upon free-trade, you must discreetly avoid promising it, and suggest that probably the privilege will be granted them as a favor." Brask, who feared lest these negotiations might cause trouble, hastened to throw a favorable light upon his own position. "You will remember," he wrote his fellow-counsellors, "that I opposed the grant of these great privileges to Lubeck, believing them injurious to the welfare of our people." Magni, in conformity with the king's injunctions, proceeded to the town of Ghent, where he was given an audience of Margaret, regent of the Netherlands. As soon as the letters of May 12, 1526, and April 18, 1527, were translated for her, she raised a number of objections, chief of which were that the latter letter did not provide that salt should be admitted free, and did not seem to open to her vessels all the Swedish ports. To these objections Magni answered that certain harbors were made ports of entry out of convenience to Gustav, and as to duties, Magni seems to have assured her that they would probably be taken off. After more palaver, Margaret signed a document accepting the offer assumed to have been made by Sweden; namely, that vessels of the emperor might enter all the rivers and harbors of Sweden, paying only the same duties that were paid by Swedish subjects, salt, however, to be admitted free. She expressed a hope, moreover, that other articles might be exempt from duty too. To this document she attached her seal, July 29, 1527.

It is particularly to be noted that Lubeck did not raise her voice against the treaty. A probable solution is that she wished beyond all else to secure her money, and felt that Sweden would be more able to meet the debt in case she were allowed to trade with Holland. All through the winter of 1527 Gustav struggled to raise funds. Some portions of the country seem to have responded freely, but in Dalarne and other northern provinces it appeared likely that the levy would end in actual revolt. In January Gustav warned the people that all responsibility in the matter lay with them. If Lubeck made war upon the kingdom, it would be because of their unwillingness to pay the debt. As a matter of fact, the Dalesmen had much reason for delay. The monarch, by his ill-judged privileges to

Lubeck, had kept the country in a state of famine, from which it now was just beginning to emerge. Many of the people were utterly devoid of means, and the new levy seemed like wringing water from a stone. This in the course of time Gustav learned, and in March he prudently suggested to his officers that the tax be modified in special cases. The Dalesmen, however, were not so easily to be appeased. Other causes of complaint were rife among them, and they formed a compact to the end that no tax should be paid until these grievances had been redressed. On the 2d of April Gustav asserted that the Dalesmen had not contributed a cent. Brask, for reasons that will be manifest later on, was in sympathy with the people, and declared: "I fear danger, for the Dalesmen are reported to be incensed, and rightfully incensed, against the king. If it lay with me, I should remit a portion of the tax rather than give occasion for this revolt." Gustav, however, was still harassed by Lubeck, and dared not take this step. As there were several matters to be straightened out in Dalarne, he summoned a general diet of the realm. The Dalesmen showing opposition, Gustav urged the people in the south of Sweden to persuade the people of Dalarne to come. "We should be glad," he urged, "if you would write to the people of Dalarne, and ask them to lay their complaints before the diet to be held in Vesterås. We shall there explain our conduct, and if our people are not satisfied, shall gladly resign the throne. The German envoys will be present, and the Dalesmen can then adopt some means to quiet their incessant demands." All efforts to persuade the Dalesmen failed. They despatched a long list of their grievances to Stockholm, but they did not attend the diet. When the other delegates came together, Gustav laid these grievances before them. The Dalesmen had complained, he said, that they were burdened with heavy taxes. If they had been more obedient, a smaller army would have been sufficient, and the taxes would not have been so heavy. He told them, further, that the whole debt occasioned by the war amounted to about one hundred thousand marks, of which sum a large portion was still unpaid. The outcome of the matter was that the delegates voted to quell the insurrection in Dalarne, and if enough money could not now be raised to pay the debt, to levy further taxes. These stringent measures were not, however, put into effect at once. Gustav was busy, in the autumn of 1527, with other things; and furthermore a dispute had arisen between himself and Lubeck as to the exact total of the debt. The year closed, therefore, with the debt still hanging over Sweden's head. The Lubeck envoys accepted all the goods and money they could get, the whole amount thus paid in 1527 being in the neighborhood of 22,800 Swedish marks.

All through this period Gustav was in constant negotiation with Fredrik. Christiern's efforts to recover the crown had been brought to a halt by the sudden collapse of Norby, and Fredrik had assumed in consequence a more aggressive attitude toward Sweden. By the treaty signed at Malmö each monarch promised to protect the interests which citizens of the other held within his realm. But the ink was scarcely dry when complaints were heard that Fredrik had failed to substantiate this clause. The most flagrant breach occurred in the case of property owned in Denmark by Margaret, sister of the king of Sweden. So great difficulty was experienced by Margaret in protecting this estate, that early in 1526 the monarch counselled her to sell it. He wrote also to certain Danish officers, and begged them to defend her rights. These exhortations proving futile, Margaret sent her agent to the spot to see what he could do. This only irritated the natives, and they fell upon the agent with their fists. It was reported, too, that the deed was ordered by an officer of Fredrik. At all events, the agent was given no redress, and Gustav, after urging Margaret's husband to appeal to Fredrik, wrote finally to the Danish king himself. He laid the whole affair before him, and declaring that he had ever upheld the rights of Danes in Sweden, urged Fredrik to investigate the matter and punish those by whom the violence had been committed. With this request the Danish monarch promised to comply; and as we find no further mention of the case, it is probable the quarrel was adjusted and the rights of Margaret maintained.

Another dispute originating in the Malmö treaty concerned the province of Viken, which lay along the Swedish frontier in the southeast part of Norway. This province had joined Gustav in the war with Christiern, and after the war was over had continued under Swedish rule. In course of time, however, the inhabitants grew eager to return once more to Norway. With a view to satisfy their longing, Gustav allowed them, early in 1526, to be governed by Norwegian law and custom. Possibly this would have appeased the natives, but Fredrik was desirous for more. He thought that Viken, being originally a province of Norway, should be ruled by him. He therefore wrote Gustav, and begged a conference to settle their respective claims. Gustav, defrauded of his rights in Gotland, answered that he would gladly hold a conference to settle all matters of dispute between them. Fredrik waited nearly six months before making his reply. He then informed Gustav that the Danish envoys had appeared in Lubeck at the day fixed for the conference, but that nothing was accomplished simply because the Swedish envoys did not come. He therefore urged Gustav to name a time and place at which the question of Viken should be settled. The Swedish monarch had learned by sad experience that a conference with Denmark meant no benefit to him. He answered that his envoys had been sent to Lubeck, as agreed, but had failed through stress of weather to reach the place of meeting on the day arranged. Gustav appears not to have cared particularly to retain the province, though he was not willing to yield it without obtaining something in return. He saw no reason why Viken should be given up to Fredrik unless Gotland should be given up to him. In answer, therefore, to repeated solicitations, he declared his readiness to meet the Danish king half-way; he would treat with him concerning Viken, but at the same time some definite conclusion must be reached about the isle of Gotland. When negotiations had reached this point, they were interrupted for the moment by a new dispute.

Ever since the fall of Kalmar, Christina's boy had been in Stockholm, under the surveillance of the king. Gustav for some reason had never liked the boy, and in April, 1527, he sent him to his mother with a reprimand, at the same time urging that he be placed for a period under the quiet influence of some rural town. This incident was the signal for another conspiracy against the crown. This time the aspirant was a gay young hostler, who conceived the desperate project of posing as the regent's son. Relying on his own audacity and on the perennial state of insurrection in the north of Sweden, he went to Dalarne with the story that he had escaped the clutches of Gustav, whose orders were that he be put to death. He then proceeded from one village to another, extolling the virtues of the young Sten Sture, and urging the people, since they had sworn allegiance to his father, to do the same to him. The support which he received was small. One or two villages were at first deceived, but the majority of them told him flatly that he lied. He therefore followed the course of earlier impostors, and betook himself to Norway. Approaching first the archbishop of Trondhem, he told his story and awoke the archbishop's interest by announcing that Gustav had fallen from the faith. It being bruited that certain of the church dignitaries were on terms of friendship with this impostor, the archbishop received him kindly, and though he refused to give him shelter, promised he would take no steps to harm him. Gustav then addressed the archbishop and the Cabinet of Norway, urging that the traitor be returned. He pointed out, moreover, that, Sten Sturehaving been married only fourteen years before, it was impossible that this traitor was his son. This argument producing no effect, Gustav prevailed upon Fredrik's emissaries, then in Stockholm, to join him in his appeal. An answer then came back from the archbishop of Trondhem that he had refused to shelter the impostor, though he had promised that he would not harm him. Since then a letter had arrived from Dalarne saying that the Swedish king was dead. The impostor had therefore collected a band of refugees in Norway, and was now once more in Sweden. With this mendacious explanation Gustav was forced to be content. The fraud had been discovered, and by the close of 1527 the insurrection in Dalarne was practically at an end.

INTERNAL ADMINISTRATION. 1525-1527.

IN most instances the stirring periods of a nation's history are not the periods in which the nation grows. Warfare, even though it end in victory, must be accompanied by loss, and the very achievements that arouse our ardor bring with them evils that long years of prosperity cannot efface. Take, as a single example, the dazzling victories of Charles XII. He was, beyond all doubt, the most successful general that Sweden ever had. One after another the provinces around the Baltic yielded to his sway, and at one time the Swedish frontiers had been extended into regions of which no man before his age had dreamt. Yet with what result? Sweden was impoverished, commerce was at a standstill, education had been neglected, and the dominions for which his people had poured out their blood during many years were lost almost in a single day. His career shows, if it shows anything, that prosperity is incompatible with war. No man can serve two masters. So long as nations are in active and continued warfare, they cannot enjoy the blessings or even the comforts that belong to them in time of peace.

A like argument may be drawn from the reign of Gustav Vasa. The early years of the Swedish Revolution were marked by bloodshed. The country was in a state of famine, superstition was universal, literature was almost without a champion, and art was practically dead. Not till the warfare ceased did people turn their thoughts to matters of education, of religion, or of other things that lend a charm to life; and even then the country was hampered during a considerable period by poverty,—an outcome of the war. It is in this last period of the Revolution—a period of peace—that the chief work of Gustav Vasa was accomplished. Then occurred the great changes in Church government and doctrine that made Lutherans out of Roman Catholics, and in place of accountability to the pope made every soul accountable to God. In the first few years of his supremacy the monarch's opposition to popery was based almost entirely on politics, but by the middle of 1525 he began openly to oppose the

Romish Church on grounds of faith.

The heaviest blow to popery was the order issued by the king in 1525 that the Scriptures be translated into Swedish. This all-important measure resulted doubtless from the general dissension that had arisen about the Word of God. If, as Luther urged, the Scriptures were our sole criterion of faith, it was obviously proper that they should be published in a form which every one could understand. Luther had already three years before translated the Bible into German, but in Swedish the only effort at a translation was in a manuscript of several centuries before, which even Brask knew only by report. Gustav, therefore, toward the middle of 1525, instructed Archbishop Magni to have a new translation made. His purpose, he affirmed, was not merely to instruct the people but to instruct the priests, for many of them were themselves incompetent to read the Latin version. As shepherds their duty was to feed Christ's flock with the Word of God; and if they failed to do so, they were unworthy of their name. This reasoning the archbishop was unable to refute. He was himself disgusted with the ignorance of his clergy, and promised Gustav that the translation should be made. Not wishing, however, to undertake too much, he devoted his attention wholly to the New Testament, dividing it into several parts and assigning the translation of different parts to different men. Matthew and the Epistle to the Romans he took himself. Mark and the Epistles to the Corinthians were assigned to Brask, while Luke and the Epistle to the Galatians were given to the Chapter of Skara, and John and the Epistle to the Ephesians to the Chapter of Strengnäs. The announcement of this choice was made to Brask on the 11th of June, and he was asked to forward his translation to Upsala by September 10, when a congress of the translators should be held to arrange the various portions into one harmonious whole. This project was not received with favor by the crafty bishop. He felt it to be the knell of popery, and in writing to Peder Galle he inveighed against it. "We marvel much," he wrote, "that the archbishop should enter this labyrinth without consulting the prelates and chapters of the Church. Every one knows that translations into the vernacular have already given rise to frequent heresy.... It is said the Bible is capable of four different interpretations. Therefore it would imperil many souls were a mere literal translation made. Moreover, laymen cannot read the Bible even if it be translated, and the clergy can understand it quite as well in Latin as in Swedish. We fear that if this translation be published while the Lutheran heresy is raging, the heresy will become more pestilent, and, new error springing up, the Church will be accused of fostering it." This letter was dated on the 9th of August. Clearly Brask's share of the translation would not be ready by September 10. The fact was, Brask had no notion of furthering the scheme. At every opportunity he raised his voice against it, and the weight of his influence was such that finally the whole project was given up. The Lutherans, however, were not disheartened. Finding that nothing could be effected through the Church, they proceeded to make a translation of their own. This was published, though without the translators' names, in 1526. It did not, of course, receive the sanction of the archbishop, but it paved the way for new reforms by checking the Roman Catholics in their scholastic doctrine and by educating the common people in the Word of God.

Brask was now openly beneath the monarch's frown. The rupture between them was becoming every day more wide, and both parties gradually grew conscious it could not be healed. Brask had never forgiven the king for sanctioning the marriage of Olaus Petri. Some six months after the event he alluded to it in a letter to Peder Galle. "I am much troubled," he declared, "that marriage is permitted to the clergy, and that no one cries out against it. I have urged the king that Petri be excommunicated for his act, that evil example may not spread, but have had only a half-hearted answer from his Majesty." While this wrong still rankled in the prelate's breast, his ire was further kindled by the monarch's evident intention to rob the Church of several of her chief estates. As an entering wedge Gustav had pastured his soldiers' horses on the rich but fallow lands belonging to the monasteries, and in some cases the officers had been billeted in the monasteries themselves. Against this practice Brask protested, and received this soothing answer: "When you say that this mode of billeting cripples the service of God, you are right, provided his service consists in feeding a body of hypocrites sunk, many of them, in licentiousness, rather than in providing protection for the common people. As to your assertion that the monasteries were not founded by the crown, and hence are not subject to our dominion, we will look into the matter, though our humble opinion is that the monasteries were originally bound to pay taxes to the crown." The argument which the monarch strove to make was this: Those monasteries which were founded by individuals comprised estates held by the donors in consideration of military service to be rendered to the crown; and so soon as the military service ended, the tenure by which the lands were held no longer existed, and the crown once more became entitled to the lands. It is difficult to feel that the monarch's view was right. In countries where there is no written law, all controversies must be determined by the law of custom, and it is certain that for centuries Swedish subjects had been allowed to dedicate for religious purposes the property which they held by military tenure of the crown. With Gustav it appears that custom was of little moment. The monasteries were wealthy, and could be encroached upon without directly injuring the people. He resolved, therefore, as soon as possible to confiscate their property, using a plausible argument if one was ready; otherwise, to close their doors by force.

In May, 1525, the king found pretext for interfering with the Dominican monks of Vesterås. That order numbered among its brothers a very large proportion of Norwegians; and one of them had assumed the generalship of the order in Sweden, contrary to the mandates of the king. This seemed an opportunity to play the patriot and at the same time secure a footing in the monastery. So Gustav wrote to the Swedish vicar-general and declared: "We understand that the conspiracy in Dalarne and other places is largely due to this man and several of the Norwegian brothers. We have therefore appointed our subject Nils Andreæ to be prior of Vesterås, trusting that he will prove a friend to Sweden, by expelling the foreigners and preventing all such conspiracies in future. We beg you also ... to punish all offenders among your brotherhood, that we be not forced to punish them ourselves."

Later in the same year Gustav asserted his claim with even more distinctness to the monastery of Gripsholm. That monastery, it will be remembered, was on the estate at one time belonging to the monarch's father. It therefore was a special object of his greed. At a meeting of the Cabinet he laid his case before them, and offered to abide by their decree. There was, of course, no question what their decree would be.

The monastery was adjudged the property of the king, and all the inmates were instructed to withdraw. This judgment naturally caused an outcry in certain quarters. So Gustav addressed the monks of Gripsholm with unctious promises, and under the mask of friendship obtained from them a written statement that they were satisfied of the justice of his claim. This document, a copy of which was filed among the royal papers, bears singular testimony to the meanness of the king. "Our title to Gripsholm Monastery," the wretched victims wrote, "has been disputed, and, the matter being laid before the Cabinet, they have determined that Gustav, as heir of the founder, is entitled to the premises. He has offered us another monastery in place of this, but we feared lest that too might some day prove to be the property of other heirs, and have requested permission to disband and retire each of us according to his own caprice. It has now been agreed that Gustav shall provide us with the money and clothing which we need, and in return that he shall be entitled to the monastery together with all the property that we have acquired." At the close of this affecting document the writers expressed their gratitude to the monarch for his generosity. Armed with this evidence of his good intentions, Gustav addressed the Dalesmen with a view to calm their wrath. "You are aware," he wrote with confidence, "that the elder Sten Sture, who was a brother of our father's mother, founded Gripsholm Monastery with property that would have descended by law to our father, and that Sten Sture induced our father to append his signature to the deed. The signature was obtained, however, only on condition that if the monastery should be unable to keep up its standing, Gripsholm and all its possessions should revert to the heirs. Hence we have good right to protest and to claim the inheritance of which our father was deprived by threats and fraud. Indeed, the good brothers have considered the matter well, and have agreed to withhold no longer property to which they have no right. We have therefore offered them another monastery.... But they have not ventured to accept it, fearing to offend the brothers already occupying it. So they have asked permission to go back to their friends and to the posts which they held before entering the monastery. This, at the desire of our Cabinet, we have granted, since we are ever ready to listen to their counsel, and we have furnished the good brothers with clothing and money to aid them. We trust they will be grateful; and to prove to you that such is the case, we enclose herewith an extract from the letter which they have written." As the deed conveying Gripsholm to the brotherhood is lost, we cannot discuss with thoroughness the merits of the case. It is enough that the monarch's action accorded with the policy which he adopted later toward all the monasteries in the land. The seizure of Gripsholm was justified, at any rate, by a show of right. Of later cases it is difficult to say even this. The Gripsholm Monastery had not been closed six months when Gustav claimed another monastery, this time in the diocese of Brask. The abbot it appears had died, and Brask was busy making a list of the monastery's property, that nothing should be lost. Gustav wrote to Brask with orders to leave the place alone. "Your fathers," he added, "did not found the monastery; and even though your predecessors in the bishopric may have founded it, they did so with money belonging to the people.... We intend, therefore, to take charge of it ourselves." To these imperative orders the wearied bishop answered: "I feel a special obligation to this monastery, since it was founded by the yearly incomes of the bishopric." This assertion, however, proved of no avail. Within a year the monastery was yielded to the crown, and one of the monarch's officers took the entire property in fee.

All things apparently conspired to bring the aged bishop to the dust. The seizure of his monastery occurred at a moment when he was in deep distress about the newly levied tax. Early in 1525 Gustav had written him to surrender all the tithes accruing in his diocese for the year last past; and following close upon this order, the royal stewards had deprived him of a right of fishery which he possessed. The hapless bishop murmured, but did not rebel. In writing to a fellow bishop, he declared: "The king has recently demanded of us all our tithes, and the chief prelates of Upland have yielded their consent. This policy appears to me unwise. I dread an outburst from the people, and scarce have courage to make the announcement to them." A few days later he said: "I have written Gustav about the tithes, but do not dare to discuss the matter seriously with the people.... Only a year ago the officers seized our tithes without consulting us. You can imagine, therefore, what the people will say to this new levy. However, if his Majesty will not countermand the order, we shall do our duty by writing and speaking to the people. The feeding of the army, which he wishes by consent of his advisers to impose upon the monasteries, we asserted at Vadstena was a foreign practice that ought never to be introduced." Despite these protests, Brask appears to have obeyed the monarch's orders. He wrote to the clergy of his diocese urging them to send their quota, and to send it quickly. "Bis dat qui cito dat," translated for the ignorant among his clergy, "He gives nothing who delays." The result was precisely what the bishop feared. The people fought against the imposition, and Brask, as a reward for his efforts, was accused by Gustav of being a party to the revolt. The charge was utterly groundless and unfair. From beginning to end the bishop's object had been to avoid friction, and finally he had sacrificed his own interests in order to prevent friction with the king. When in January, 1526, it was once more voted that the tithes be given to the crown, he wrote to all his clergy urging them immediately to obey. Gustav, however, would not be appeased; and a parishioner claiming that the bishop had withheld some jewels that belonged to her, Gustav, without examining the matter, wrote to Brask: "The law, as we interpret it, gives you no power to take high-handed measures of this sort." A few days later Brask asserted: "The royal officers are beginning to enter upon the possessions of the Church, much to the displeasure of the people." What he alluded to particularly was the acts of Arvid Vestgöte, who had seized Church tithes and committed every sort of violence to the priests in Öland. Against this Brask protested, and before the year was over Vestgöte was removed. By this time the spirit of the aged bishop was well-nigh broken. In answer to a summons from Gustav in 1526, he wrote the king: "Though shattered by illness and the infirmities of age, I will obey your orders with all the haste I can, provided the weather or my death does not prevent me."

Early in 1526, at one of the public fairs, an enthusiast came forward and announced in public that a leading Lutheran in Stockholm was preaching heresy, and that the king himself had violated old Church customs in his food and drink. This silly assertion burst like a bomb upon the town, and for a short period there was danger that the fanaticism of the year before would be renewed. However, the excitement soon died away; and Gustav, when he heard of it, declared the story to be a fabrication. "Would to God," he wrote, "that people would examine into their own lives and not borrow trouble about the lives of others! Let them first pluck the beam out of their own eye, and then they can see clearly to pluck the mote out of their brother's eye." Lutheranism had by this time attained so general acceptance that the monarch deemed it unnecessary to offer arguments in its support. In August, 1526, Laurentius Andreæ forwarded to the archbishop of Trondhem the New Testament in Swedish, and added that some two or three hundred copies of the edition were still unsold, and could be had if he desired them. This wide-spread distribution of the Scriptures produced its natural effect. The flame of theological discord that had been slumbering for a year broke out afresh. Brask, as an offset to the new translation, interpreted into Swedish some tracts composed in Germany against the Lutherans; and the monarch, hearing of this move, sent off a letter commanding the aged bishop to desist. "Report has reached us, venerable father," he began, "that you have translated into Swedish certain proclamations of the emperor against the doctrines now current, ... and that you have circulated them among the common people. We are well aware that these proclamations are used to cast aspersions on us, since we are not so zealous as he is in opposition to these doctrines. It is, therefore, our desire and our command that you be patient, and send hither certain scholars from your cathedral to prove that anything is taught here other than the holy gospel. They shall be given a fair hearing, and may postulate their views without prejudice in any way. And if they can prove that any one preaches unchristian doctrine, he shall be punished. Furthermore, we object to having a printing-press established in Söderköping, lest it may do injury to the one established here." Gustav was determined that the enemies of Luther should defend their faith. The disputation between Galle and Olaus Petri two years before had been unsystematic, and had produced no permanent effect. So the king resolved to force the parties to debate again. This time he put down in writing certain questions, and sent them to the leading prelates of the land, with orders to forward him their answers. The questions were similar to those already raised; among them being these: Whether we may reject all teaching of the Fathers and all Church customs that are unsupported by the Word of God; whether the dominion of the pope and his satellites is for or against Christ; whether any authority can be found in the Bible for monastic life; whether any revelation is to be relied on other than that recorded in the Bible; whether the saints are to be considered patrons, or in any way are mediators between ourselves and God. Gustav intended that when the answers were all received, a public hearing should be had, and every prelate given an opportunity to refute the doctrines of his opponents. Some of the Roman Catholics, however, refused to enter the arena. Brask, in writing to the monarch, declared his clergy to be satisfied with their present doctrines, and unwilling to discuss them publicly. The bishop also wrote to Galle, hoping to dissuade him from the contest. But Galle, it appears, was eager for the fray. He put his answers down in writing, and sent them to the king. Other prelates, it is reported, did the same. The contest, however, presumably from lack of combatants, did not succeed. Petri therefore took the written answers filed by Galle, and printed them in book form, along with comments by himself. This book does little credit either to Petri or to the general intelligence of his time. Should any one ask proof that we are more rational creatures than our fathers, he can do no better than study in Petri's book the controversy that raged between the intellectual giants of Sweden at the close of 1526. Of the positions taken by the two contestants, Petri's was certainly less consistent than that of his opponent. Galle declared explicitly: "Not everything done by the Apostles or their successors is written in the Scriptures;" and on matters concerning which the Bible does not speak we must obey the practices handed down by the Apostles through the Church. Petri, while granting that many Fathers were inspired, declared we must not follow their instructions, "lest we be led away by the devil;" and yet the Bible, compiled from various sources by the Fathers, he held should be implicitly obeyed. In the light of recent scholarship, both combatants were wrong. The Bible is no more intelligible without a knowledge of its history than is the teaching of the Fathers without a knowledge of the Bible.

The contest has its chief value in the opportunity that it gives us to study the methods of the king. From first to last it was a blow at popery and the temporal supremacy of Rome. Each question was worded with the very purpose of offering insult to the Church. Take for example the second question: whether the dominion of the pope and his satellites is for or against Christ. The monarch could not have thrown the question into a more irritating form. Certainly Galle showed forbearance in arguing the point at all. His answer was an appeal to history. From the days of Gregory popes had enjoyed vast riches along with temporal power; this showed that they were justified in possessing wealth. Galle's logic on the subject is not altogether clear. Petri's was somewhat better. Christ had distinctly told the Apostles that his kingdom was not of this world, and Paul had declared that the Apostles were not to be masters but servants. Petri then broke out into a tirade against his opponent's view. What right, he asked, had Galle to set up Gregory against Christ and Paul? "What authority has he to expound the Word of God according to the deeds of petty men? Rather, I conceive, are the deeds of men to be judged according to the Word of God." To an assertion by Galle that the Church had held temporal power for the last twelve centuries, Petri answered: "For that matter, the Word of God has lasted still longer than twelve centuries.... However, the question is not how old the thing is, but how right it is. The devil is old, and none the better for it. That bishops are temporal lords is contrary to the Word of God; and the longer they have been so, the worse for them. Princes and emperors have granted the pope vast privileges, by which in course of time he has become their master, till now all men bow down and kiss his feet. Where he was given an inch, he has taken an ell.... Christ told Saint Peter to feed his lambs. But the popes with their satellites have long since ceased to feed Christ's lambs, and for centuries have done naught but fleece and slaughter them, not acting like faithful shepherds, but like ravening wolves." This vehement language must have pleased the king. If bishops were not entitled to worldly goods, it was an easy task to confiscate their property to the crown. A like incentive called forth the question: whether any authority can be found in the Bible for monastic life. The question, in that form, permitted no reference to the Fathers. So Galle cited the command of Jesus: "Go, sell all that thou hast, and give to the poor;" and he further commended monastic life as a step on the way to heaven. Petri replied that monks did not sell all they had and give to the poor, but clung fast to their possessions, bringing vast treasures into the monasteries with them.

The disputation, while strengthening the hands of Petri, caused a momentary shout of opposition to the king. The cry arose that he was introducing strange and novel faiths. His faiths perhaps were novel, but they were not strange. The strangest feature in the matter was the position taken by the king. By this time, there can be no question, he was at heart with Luther; yet, judging from his own assertions, he was a firm defender of the Church. The king's duplicity, of course, is easily explained. He wished to rob the Roman Catholics of their power without incurring their ill-will. He intended to reform their doctrines, and at the same time spread abroad the notion that these doctrines had reformed themselves. Some time before the disputation, he had written to the north of Sweden to explain his views. "Dear friends," he courteously began, "we hear that numerous reports have spread among you to the effect that we have countenanced certain novel doctrines taught by Luther. No one can prove, however, that we have countenanced aught except the teaching of God and his Apostles. For the faith given us by our fathers we shall battle so long as life remains, and die, as our fathers died before us, in the faith. The seditious libels spread by Sunnanväder and his followers have occasioned all the injury that has fallen in days gone by upon this kingdom, as every reasonable man must know. Doubtless there are among the clergy as well as among the people many who are conscious of what they ought to do. But certain monks and priests have raised this cry against us, chiefly for the reason that we have denounced their ambitious projects and their unrighteous dealings toward the people. If any person owes them anything, they withhold from him the sacrament, and thus wring his money from him against the law of God.... Again, if a man kills a bird or catches a fish on the Sabbath day, they fine him in behalf of their bishop. This they have no right to do unless the act is committed during church service, when the culprit should have been listening to the Word of God. Again, whenever a priest has wronged a layman, the layman is practically without a remedy. He ought, however, to have the same remedy as the priest. Again, if a layman kills a priest, he is at once put under the ban, whereas if a priest kills a layman, he is not put under the ban. Yet God has forbidden priests to kill laymen as well as laymen to kill priests, making no difference in fact between them, but commanding all men to be affectionate and peaceable toward one another. Finally, if a priest dies intestate, his heirs lose their inheritance and his property is taken by the bishop. Even the crown estates, which they know we are bounden by our oath of office to protect, they have confiscated, and now they proclaim that we have introduced new faiths and doctrines taught by Luther. All we have done, as you already know, is to command them not to carry on their ambitious practices to the ruin of our realm." This explanation did not wholly calm the peasants; and when they found Gustav holding another contest over their religious tenets, their suspicions were aroused again. Gustav determined, therefore, that he must take some drastic measure to prevent revolt. What he needed was a vote of all the people to support his views. So he issued a proclamation in January, 1527, informing the whole country that, since he was reported to be introducing new beliefs, he should soon summon a general diet to discuss the more important matters of belief, particularly the overweening power of the pope.

To this serious step Gustav was impelled by several things. In the first place he desired to fortify himself against the pope. During the last three years the pope had practically been without authority in Sweden. Gustav had selected as his bishops men whose actions he was able to control, and the pope had deprived himself of even the semblance of authority by refusing to confirm them. However, the nominal supremacy of Rome was not yet shaken off; and until it was so, there was constant danger that her actual supremacy would revive. The monarch's chief anxiety concerned Archbishop Magni. That prelate owed his appointment mainly to the pliability of his temper, and to the assumption on the monarch's part that he would prove a ready tool. In this assumption Gustav had soon discovered he was wrong. Magni, though of pliant temper, was a thorough Papist, and, as time went on, displayed a growing tendency to oppose the king. In consequence he gradually fell from favor, till he became an object of open distrust. The earliest evidence of this feeling appeared in 1525, when Magni, as one of the envoys sent to Lubeck, was warned to take no action without the acquiescence of the other envoys. This mandate was issued from a fear lest Magni should encourage Lubeck to raise her voice against the spread of Lutheranism in the Swedish kingdom. How far this fear was justified, it is difficult to say. As Lubeck had not yet embraced the Reformation, she doubtless sympathized in some degree with Magni, but there is not the slightest evidence that Magni was unfaithful to the king. In February, of the following year, when Magni was starting for the Norwegian frontier to administer the rite of confirmation, he wrote the archbishop of Trondhem that he would like to meet him and discuss the dangerous condition of the Church. Gustav, hearing of the contents of this letter, was aroused again. The archbishop of Trondhem had given offence by harboring Swedish refugees, andMagni's simple letter caused the monarch to believe that the two archbishops were, as he expressed it, "in secret negotiation." Some two months later, Gustav being in the archbishop's palace, a stately feast was given in his honor. This only added to the feud. The monarch was incensed to find that Magni was capable of such display. Hot words ensued between them, and finally the archbishop was arrested and conveyed to Stockholm. There he was charged with conspiracy against the king. Certain letters that had passed between him and the Roman Catholics of Germany were produced; and though they showed no evidence of fraud, the archbishop was remanded to his prison to await the further disposition of his case. Never was greater injustice done a worthy man. There was not a scintilla of evidence against him. He was a generous, kindly, single-minded prelate, and the only reason for this cruelty was that he had no sympathy with the methods of the king. After some months in prison he was released upon the pretext of an embassy to Poland. Nobody could be ignorant what this pretext meant. He was to be an exile from his native land. He sailed from Sweden in the autumn of 1526, never to return. By such ignoble practices the monarch cleared his path.

After the banishment of Archbishop Magni, Gustav gave free rein to his ambition. The principal object of his greed was still the monasteries and convents. The practice of quartering his soldiers in them was by this time accepted as a necessary evil. But in August, 1526, he raised a new pretension. The provost of the Åbo Chapter having died, its members had chosen another in his stead, and had begun to distribute his property in accordance with a will that he had left, when a letter came from Sweden ordering them to stop. After expressing surprise that they should have chosen a provost without consulting him, Gustav added: "We learn that your last provost left a large amount of property by his testament to those persons to whom he wished to have it go. It is clear, however, that it would do more good if given to the public, since the kingdom is in a state of distress brought on by the long-protracted war against King Christiern. We therefore command you, after distributing the legacies given to his family and friends as well as the poor, to hand the balance over to us to pay the nation's debt." Against this high-handed measure there was no redress. It was but part of a policy by this time well established in the monarch's mind. Some six months later, the burgomaster and Council of Arboga wrote Gustav that affairs in their monastery were managed in a very slipshod way; that when a brother died, the prior took possession of his estate, and the monastery itself got nothing for it. To prevent this state of things, Gustav sent an officer to take up quarters in the monastery and send him a list of all the property he could find. "You will discover also," he declared, "some chests belonging to foreign monks. Take a look at them, and see what they contain." This letter, it should be remembered, was not intended for the public eye. Gustav was careful to keep his actions dark, and, the monks of Arboga being accused of secreting certain treasures, the royal officer was instructed to make a diligent investigation, but to lay his hands on nothing until he received more positive commands. He was careful, also, that his practice of confiscating Church property should not be taken as an excuse for private individuals to do the same. In one case, where such a thing was done, he denounced the perpetrator in the strongest terms. Moreover, when the monasteries began to murmur against the soldiers quartered with them, he sent out an open letter to them, declaring that he had instructed his officers to be as courteous to them as they could. It may be noted, however, that he showed no signs of mitigating their distress.

Early in 1527 Gustav determined that the crucial moment for the Reformation had arrived. Dalarne, as usual, was in a state of insurrection, and every effort which he made to check the Church called forth a storm of imprecations from the northern provinces. The tax imposed upon the Dalesmen being still withheld, it was particularly necessary that the insurrection should be stayed. In February, therefore, Gustav wrote a letter to appease the people. "Dear friends," began the monarch, "we understand a report is spread among the people that some new creed is preached here to the dishonor of God, the Virgin, and the saints. Before God we declare this rumor to be false. Nothing is here preached or taught except the pure word of God, as given by Christ to his Apostles.... It is indeed true, that denunciations have been heard in public against the vice and avarice of the clergy, and against the flagrant abuse of their privileges. They have oppressed the ignorant with excommunication, withholding of the sacrament, and all sorts of impositions. Wholly without authority from Holy Writ, they have imposed their Romish indulgences upon you, carrying vast treasures of gold and silver out of the kingdom, thus weakening our realm and impoverishing our people, while the high prelates have grown rich and haughty toward the lords and princes from whom these very privileges were derived.... We therefore urge you all by your sworn allegiance, not to be deceived by false rumors about us, doubting nothing that we shall move heaven and earth to promote your interests. And we beg you earnestly to believe that we are as good a Christian as any living man, and shall do our utmost to promote the Christian faith." Every one could see that this assertion was intended to persuade the Dalesmen to pay the newly levied tax. As the effort proved without avail, the monarch called a general diet to be held on the 9th of June, the object being, as he declared, to put an end to the dissension that had arisen in divine affairs. Later, the diet was postponed to June 15, and, to appease the Dalesmen, was ordered to be held in Vesterås, a city that was near their province.

Before the day appointed for the diet, a long list of their grievances was drawn up by the Dalesmen and sent to Stockholm to the king. To these complaints Gustav issued a reply, in which he strove to pacify the malcontents and thus obtain their presence at the diet. The complaints themselves are somewhat trivial, but the monarch's answer is important as an instance of his peculiar power in avoiding discord without directly compromising his affairs. To their murmur at the abolition of the mint in Vesterås, and the scarcity of coins of small denominations, he answered that the mint was closed because the mines adjacent were no longer worked; so soon as the mines in question should be opened he would reinstate the mint, and moreover he would please them by issuing small coins. As to the complaint of heavy taxes, the Cabinet were responsible for that. He would say, however, that he did not contemplate any further tax. The practice of billeting in the towns and monasteries was made necessary by the paucity of land about the royal castles, but this necessity he hoped would not exist much longer. The charge of reducing the number of monasteries and churches he denied. He had not closed a single monastery except Gripsholm, which was the property of his father and had been made a monastery against his father's will. To the ludicrous charge that he was planning to restore Archbishop Trolle, he made a flat denial. One thing, he said, was certain,—those who favored Trolle favored Christiern; he could scarce be charged with that. Finally, the Dalesmen complained of Luther's teachings, particularly the doctrines that were taught in Stockholm and the practice of allowing Swedish chants and hymns. To this he could say only that he had ordered nothing to be preached except the Word of God; and as to Swedish chants, he could see no reason for punishing in Stockholm what was permitted in all other portions of the kingdom; it was certainly better to praise God in a language that everybody understood than in Latin, which no one understood. "I wonder much," he said in closing, "that the Dalesmen trouble themselves concerning matters of which they have no knowledge. It would be wiser to leave the discussion of these things to priests and scholars.... I do not believe, however, that these complaints are made of your own free will, but rather at the instigation of certain priests and monks, whose desire is to keep the truth unknown." This sentence with which he closed contains the pith of the entire letter. The monarch felt that in the coming contest the opposing parties were to be the Church and State. He endeavored, therefore, by every means to win the Dalesmen to his side. Letters were despatched to Dalarne from various portions of the realm, to instruct the peasants that if they persisted in their opposition to Gustav, they would have to fight alone. The Dalesmen, however, were no more influenced by threats than by persuasion. They stood firm in their determination; and when the diet assembled on the 24th of June, no delegates from Dalarne appeared.

The Diet of Vesterås is the bulwark of the Swedish Reformation. It is the first embodiment in the Swedish law of the reforms of Martin Luther. Gustav had been making ready for this diet ever since the day of his election, and at last the opportunity was ripe. One by one the prelates that were hostile to his views had been removed; and Brask, the only man of strength that still held out against him, was tottering to the grave. His enemies abroad had been by this time silenced, and except in the little province of Dalarne, Sweden was at peace. It was this revolt among the Dalesmen that served as a pretext for the diet. Gustav was too shrewd a politician to make an open avowal of his aim. He announced that the purpose of the diet was to quell the constant riots in the realm, and hinted with mock innocence that he wished also to end the dissension that had arisen in matters of the Church. Among the persons who answered to the summons we find the names of four bishops, including Brask, together with representatives from Upsala and all the other Chapters excepting Åbo. Beside these, there were present one hundred and forty-four of the nobility (of whom sixteen were Cabinet members), thirty-two burghers, one hundred and five peasants, and fourteen delegates from the mining districts. The king's design had been made manifest before the diet met; for on the previous Sunday, at a banquet given by him to the delegates already arrived in Vesterås, he had taken especial pains to show the bishops that their temporal supremacy was at an end. Despising every venerated custom, he had ranged about himself the higher members of the nobility, and had consigned the bishops to an inferior position. The affront thus put upon them galled them to the quick, and on the following day they held a secret meeting to discuss their wrongs. All of the bishops present excepting Brask discerned the hopelessness of their cause, and advocated a humble submission to the monarch's will. But Brask was boiling over with indignation. He sprang to his feet and shouted that they must be mad. If the king wanted to deprive them of their rights by force, he might do so. But they ought never to consent to such a course, lest they might thereby offend the Holy See. In times gone by, princes had frequently attempted the same thing that Gustav was attempting now, but the thunders of the Vatican had always overwhelmed them. If the bishops now should fall away from their allegiance to the pope, their only refuge would be gone. They would become mere puppets of the king, afraid to speak a word in favor of their old prerogatives. These sentiments of Brask's were listened to with favor. The warmth with which he spoke produced its natural effect, and before the prelates parted they drew up a set of "protests," as they called them, agreeing never to abandon the pope or accept a single article of Luther's teaching. To these "protests" the prelates all attached their seals; and fifteen years afterward the document was discovered under the floor of Vesterås Cathedral, with all the seals attached.

Directly following this secret session of the prelates, the general diet assembled in the grand hall of the monastery. The proceedings opened with a laborious address from Gustav,—his secretary, Laurentius Andreæ, acting as spokesman for the king. This address reviewed the entire history of the monarch's reign. He began by thanking his subjects for their presence at the diet, and went on to remind them that he had already more than once expressed his willingness to resign the crown. Nothing had induced him to retain it except their earnest prayer. He had therefore striven, night and day, to promote the welfare of his people, and in return for all his labors insurrection had sprung up on every hand, till now, the Dalesmen having once again rebelled, he was determined that he would no longer be their king. They charged him now with imposing heavy taxes, with keeping up the price of food, with billeting his soldiers in the towns and monasteries, with robbing churches and confiscating religious property, with favoring new creeds and sanctioning new customs. All these charges were untrue. He had commanded that nothing should be preached except the Word of God; but his orders had not been obeyed, for the people preferred to cling to their ancient customs, whether right or wrong. As it was impossible, under the present system, to avoid continual rebellion, he wished to retire from the government. If they desired him to remain, some method must be found to increase the royal income. He was at present wholly unable to pay the expenses of his army, for war had grown to be a much more costly matter than it was in former days. Other expenses, too, were very heavy. The cost of embassies to foreign powers was a serious drain upon his revenue. Moreover, the royal castles had all sunk into decay and must be rebuilt; and if he married the daughter of some foreign prince, a vast outlay would be required. The nobility also were impoverished through constant warfare, and were calling on the crown for aid. His present income was twenty-four thousand marks per annum, while his expenses in round numbers amounted to sixty thousand marks.

At the close of this address Gustav called upon the knights and bishops to reply. Although the monarch's speech had not in terms denounced the bishops, it was clear to all men that his purpose was to humble them. The duty of making answer, therefore, naturally fell to Brask. That venerable prelate rose, and with his usual complaisance declared that, having sworn allegiance to his gracious lord the king, he felt in duty bound to honor his commands. He had, however, by his oath of office promised to do nothing contrary to the will of Rome; and since the pope had ordered him and the other prelates to defend all property, whether real or personal, of the holy Church, they must not consent to sacrifice their rights. But he would promise that any deacons, priests, or monks who might devise tricks or superstitious practices not prescribed by their superiors, should be ordered to desist and should be punished.

At this, Gustav demanded of the Cabinet and nobility whether they were satisfied with the answer. As none seemed eager to defend the monarch's cause, Gustav took the floor himself and said: "I have no further desire, then, to be your king. Verily I had not counted on such treatment at your hands. I now no longer wonder at the perversity of the people, since they have such men as you for their advisers. Have they no rain? They lay the blame on me. Have they no sun? Again they lay the blame on me. When hard times come, hunger, disease, or whatever it may be, they charge me with it, as if I were not man, but God. This is your gratitude to me for bringing corn and rye and malt at great expense and trouble from foreign lands, that the poor of Sweden might not starve. Yea, though I labor for you with my utmost power both in spiritual and in temporal affairs, you would gladly see the axe upon my neck; nay, you would be glad to strike the blow yourselves. I have borne more labor and trouble both at home and abroad than any of you can know or understand,—and all because I am your king. You would now set monks and priests and all the creatures of the pope above my head, though we have little need of these mighty bishops and their retinue. In a word, you all would lord it over me; and yet you elected me your king. Who under such circumstances would desire to govern you? Not the worst wretch in hell would wish the post, far less any man. Therefore I, too, refuse to be your king. I cast the honor from me, and leave you free to choose him whom you will. If you can find one who will continue ever to please you, I shall be glad. Be so considerate, however, as to let me leave the land. Pay me for my property in the kingdom, and return to me what I have expended in your service. Then I declare to you I will withdraw never to return to my degenerate, wretched, and thankless native land."

After this burst of passion, the monarch strode in anger from the hall. He had studied his position well, and knew that his opponents in the end must yield. No sooner had he left the meeting than his secretary rose and sought to bring the members to the monarch's views. "My good men," he began, "let us arrive at some conclusion in this matter, seeking aid from God. It is a weighty question that we are to answer, and one upon which hangs the welfare of our people. You heard the king say truly there were but two courses open. One was to follow his request, imploring him to be our leader hereafter as heretofore; the other was to choose the king's successor." But the delegates continued silent, and adjourned toward evening without putting the question to a vote.

During three whole days the deadlock lasted. From the inactivity of the king's adherents, it would seem that they were acting according to advice. Gustav wished to force his enemies' hand. It was clear to everybody that the blessings conferred by him on Sweden were beyond all praise, and he was confident that no one would be rash enough to talk seriously about selecting another for the throne. His object was to wait until the patience of his enemies was exhausted, in the hope that ultimately the offer of a compromise should come from them. If such methods of procedure are to be allowed, it must be granted that the monarch's policy was shrewd. During the three days following his stormy action in the diet, he kept himself in the castle, entertaining his trusty courtiers and feigning utter indifference to what was going on outside. On the very day after his withdrawal, this independent policy began to tell. The bishop of Strengnäs was apparently the first to waver. He appreciated the folly of longer holding out against the king, and rose to say that he regarded such a step as fraught with danger. Something must be done, he said, without delay. To put aside Gustav and elect another king was simply childish, and to buy up all his property would be impossible. While he wished the clergy's rights to be protected, he asked for nothing that would be a detriment to the realm. Matters in general were now improving, and the future apparently was bright. If Gustav should be permitted to withdraw, nations that had ever coveted the kingdom would no longer leave it unmolested. The effect of these words was in a measure lost through a wrangle that ensued between Laurentius Petri and the Papist champion, Peder Galle. What they were fighting over, no one knew, for Petri made his argument in Swedish for the benefit of the people, and Galle would not answer in anything but Latin. Nothing had been accomplished, therefore, when the disputation ceased. And the morning and the evening were the second day.

When the diet once more came together, the battle opened with replenished strength. By this time the peasantry and burghers had pretty generally sided with the king, and threats were heard that, if the knights persisted in their stubborn purpose, they would be made to suffer for it. This language proved more efficacious than persuasion. The knights and bishops could agree upon no policy, nor upon a leader. They were terrified, moreover, by the preponderance in number of their foes. As a consequence, they gradually weakened, till at last the delegates all voted to obey the monarch's will. Andreæ and Petri were therefore chosen to approach Gustav and inform him that the delegates would now consent to his requests. Gustav then indulged once more his love of masquerade. He feigned reluctance to accept the proffered honor, and scorned the delegates who came to him upon their knees. One after another the recalcitrant members grovelled in the dust before him, and begged that he would show them mercy. This was the sort of ceremony that the monarch loved. He kept his enemies in their humble posture till his vanity was glutted, and then declared that he would go before the diet on the following day.

Gustav was at last in a position to dictate to the diet. The opportunity for which he had been longing since his first acceptance of the crown was now at hand. He had won an unconditional victory over every one of his opponents, and he was minded to use this victory for all that it was worth. It is matter of regret that practically no account is given us of the steps by which the measures that he sought to have enacted were attained. This very meagreness, however, is strong evidence that the measures were enacted without much friction. Apparently, the only object of the delegates now was to suit their action to the monarch's will. They therefore adopted as their guiding star the propositions with which the diet had been opened by the king, and formulated a set of answers in conformity therewith. These answers were drawn respectively by the Cabinet and nobility, by the burghers and mountaineers, and by the common people. It is worthy of more than passing notice that no answer was presented by the clergy. Indeed, the clergy appear to have been regarded in the light of victims. The whole object of the diet was to crush the Church, and the clergy were not permitted even to have a hand in the proceedings. The monarch's notion was to give the clergy no voice whatever in the diet, but after the lay delegates had formulated their resolves, to force the bishops to issue a proclamation certifying their assent.

It seems desirable to describe in brief the answers which the different classes of delegates presented. The Cabinet and nobility began by promising that, if the rebellion in Dalarne were not already quelled, they would use every measure in their power to attain that end. They were satisfied with the monarch's seizure of Gripsholm. They deemed it proper, since the royal rents were small, that Gustav be at liberty to grant the monasteries of the land as fiefs, but not, however, to expel the monks. In order to increase the wealth of the nobility, they advocated that all property granted by former noblemen to churches or monasteries since 1454 revert to the donors' heirs, though not until such heirs should prove their title. To augment the crown's resources, they believed the bishops, chapters, and cathedrals should surrender to the king all that portion of their income which they did not absolutely need. No one should be permitted to preach falsehood or anything beyond the simple Word of God, and old Church customs ought to be maintained.

The burghers and mountaineers gave their answer in a similar vein. They begged Gustav to remain their king, and promised to defend him with their blood. They would express no opinion concerning Dalarne till the Dalesmen who were going thither should bring back their report. Since the monks were clearly at the bottom of the trouble, no monk should be permitted to leave his monastery more than twice a year. Gustav should be given the right of billeting whenever it were necessary. Before deciding about the new beliefs they wished to hear a disputation on the subject. As the rents of the nobility and crown had been diminished by the Church, the Church ought certainly to restore them; and the mode of restoration should be determined by Gustav and his Cabinet. The royal castles having been demolished, the prelates should surrender theirs until the castles belonging to the crown could be rebuilt. Finally, from that day forth no bishop ought to send to Rome for confirmation.

The answer of the common people began with a promise that they would go to Dalarne and inflict punishment upon the traitors; and since many monks were in the habit of inciting the people to rebel, it seemed desirable that they be permitted to leave their monasteries only twice each year. Gustav might quarter his soldiers in the monasteries whenever it was necessary. The churches and monasteries near Stockholm, having in times past given shelter to the enemy, should be torn down and their materials used to repair the city walls. All matters of creed they were willing to leave to the bishops and prelates, but asked that a disputation on these subjects might be had in presence of representatives of the people. The king should have authority to increase his revenue in the way that seemed to him most fitting. The king might take the bishops' castles till his own could be rebuilt. The proper disposition of the Church incomes they were content to leave to the king and his Cabinet.

One cannot but be startled by the revolutionary tendency of these replies. Never before had such a thing been dreamt of as the surrender of all the bishops' castles to the crown. Gustav must have been bewildered by his own audacity. Within four days the diet that had come together puffed up by a consciousness of its own magnificence, had sunk into a position of absolute servility. Things had been granted by the delegates which, when the diet opened, Gustav had not even dared to ask. The very mode in which the votes were taken and the acts were passed, shows how completely everybody answered to the monarch's nod. Instead of the answers being submitted to a general vote, they were laid before the Cabinet to be passed upon by them. In defiance of every precedent, the Cabinet usurped the right to clothe the diet's sentiment in language of their own. The result was a decree promulgated in the diet's name and celebrated in Swedish history as the Vesterås Recess. By this decree the delegates asserted, every one of them, that they would do their utmost to punish all conspiracies against the king. They declared, moreover, that as the royal incomes were but meagre, the monasteries and churches must come to the relief, and, to prevent all danger, no bishop should keep up a larger retinue than the king allowed. All bishops and cathedrals, with their chapters, must hand over to the king all income not absolutely necessary for their support. Since many monasteries were dilapidated and their lands were lying waste, an officer must be appointed by the crown to keep them up and hand over all their rents not needed for that purpose to the crown. The nobility were declared entitled to all property that had passed from their ancestors to the Church since 1454. Finally, Gustav was ordered to summon the two factions in the Church to hold a disputation in presence of the diet, and the members promised to quell the outcry that had arisen against Gustav and to punish the offenders.

It is reported that something in the nature of a disputation was now held. But its significance, at any rate, was small. The bishops and their clergy were to all intents and purposes without a voice; and ere the diet closed, a set of resolutions had been passed which did away with all necessity for further disputation. These so-called "Vesterås Ordinantia" were even more far-reaching than the "Vesterås Recess." Since they are the touchstone of the modern Swedish faith, the reader will pardon prolixity if I give them all. They are as follows: (1) Vacancies in the parish-churches are to be filled by the bishop of the diocese. If, however, he appoints murderers, drunkards, or persons who cannot or will not preach the Word of God, the king may expel them and appoint other priests who are more fit. (2) Where a parish is poor, two of them may be joined together, though not if such a step would be an injury to the Word of God. (3) All bishops shall furnish the king with a schedule of their rents and incomes of every kind. From these schedules he shall determine the relative proportions for them to keep and to hand over to the crown. (4) A similar course shall be pursued with regard to the cathedrals and chapters. (5) Auricular confession must be given up as already commanded, and an account must be rendered to the king of all fines imposed. (6) An account must also be rendered to the king of all fees received for remitting the ban, and bishops with their officers must not inflict the ban for petty offences, as has been often done hitherto. (7) Bishops shall have authority to determine as to the legality of marriages, and may grant divorces, but an account shall be rendered to the king of all fees received therefor. (8) Fees for weddings, funerals, and churchings, may be taken as provided in the Church ordinances, but no more. (9) Since it has been decreed that the king and not the bishop is to receive all fines imposed in cases within ecclesiastical jurisdiction, the provosts may hereafter hold court just as the bishops have done hitherto, and shall render an account of their doings to the king. (10) For desecration of holy days no penalty is to be imposed on those who have been tilling the ground, or fishing, or catching birds, but persons discovered hunting or quarrelling shall be fined. (11) Priests shall be subject to temporal laws and temporal courts, in all disputes, of their own or of their churches, concerning property, torts, or contracts, and shall pay to the king the same penalties as laymen. But all complaints against the clergy for non-fulfilment of their priestly duties shall be laid before the bishop. (12) If a priest and layman come to blows, one shall not be placed under the ban any more than the other, for God has forbidden priests to quarrel as well as laymen. Both shall suffer for their acts according to the laws of the land. (13) Since it has been found that mendicant monks spread lies and deceit about the country, the royal stewards are to see that they do not remain away from their monasteries more than five weeks every summer and five weeks every winter. Every monk must get a license from the steward or burgomaster before he goes out, and return it when he comes back. (14) Monks who receive rents shall not go out to beg at all. (15) When a priest dies, the bishop is not to defraud the priest's heirs of their inheritance. Priests shall be bound, in regard to their wills, by the same law as other people. (16) If a man has sexual intercourse with a woman to whom he is engaged, he shall not be punished, since they are already married in the eye of God. (17) No person who is infirm shall be compelled by priests to make a will. (18) The sacrament shall not be withheld from any one for debt or other reason. The church or priest has a remedy in court. (19) Fines for adultery and fornication belong to the king, not to the bishop. (20) The Gospel shall hereafter be taught in every school. (21) Bishops shall consecrate no priest who is incompetent to preach the Word of God. (22) No one shall be made a prelate, canon, or prebend unless he has been recommended by the king, or his name submitted to the king.

These ordinances were practically a signal for the death of popery. They not only transferred to the king the rich emoluments on which for centuries the bishops had grown fat; they transferred also to him a right to superintend the actions of ecclesiastical authorities in matters appertaining to the Church. It is hardly credible that so vast an object should have been attained without more friction, and that it was attained is a lasting testimony to the shrewdness of the king. We may sneer at the childish indignation with which Gustav strode forth from the diet, but the fact remains that this pretended indignation gained its end. Above all else, Gustav knew the character of his people. They were particularly prone to sentiment. A few sham tears or an exuberant display of wrath had more effect upon them than the most sagacious argument that the monarch could employ. His policy, therefore, was to stir their feelings, and then withdraw to watch their feelings effervesce. It is not too much to say that no monarch has ever in so short a time effected greater change in sentiment than Gustav effected among the members of this diet.

Before the delegates departed, a letter was issued by all the bishops present, and by representatives of the absent bishops, declaring to the people that Gustav had portrayed in graphic terms the evil inflicted on the crown in former times by bishops; and that the lay members had voted, to prevent such danger in the future, that the bishops' retinues should be limited thereafter by the king, and that all their superfluous rents and castles, as well as the superfluous rents of the cathedrals and chapters, should be surrendered to the crown. "To this," the humbled prelates added, "we could not, even if we would, object, for we wish to dispel the notion that our power and castles are a menace to the realm. We shall be satisfied whether we are rich or poor." To one who reads between these lines, it is easy to discern the language of the king. He also wrote, above his own name, to the people, informing them that the diet had been held; and for details of the proceedings he referred them to a letter which the Cabinet had penned.

There was one man on whom the diet of Vesterås had fallen like a clap of thunder from on high. His cherished dream of finally restoring Romanism to her old position in the eyes of men was now no more. The knell of popery had been sounded, and nothing remained for the aged bishop but despair. True to the spirit of the ancient Church, he had looked askance on every effort to discuss her faith. The doctrines handed down through centuries appeared to him so sacred that in his eyes it was sacrilege to open them again. In answer to the monarch's oft-repeated counsel that the Church reform her doctrines, he had steadily asserted his unwillingness to take that step, "for these new doctrines," he declared, "have been investigated frequently in other countries and have been condemned. No man of wisdom, I believe, will champion a doctrine that is contrary to the mandates of the Christian Church." This constant opposition on the part of Brask had brought him more and more beneath the monarch's frown. Gustav let no opportunity escape to add humiliation to the venerable bishop. On one occasion Brask unwittingly had consecrated as a nun a woman who formerly had been betrothed; and when the woman later left the convent to become her lover's wife, the bishop placed them both beneath the ban. This act called forth a condemnation from the king. "The bearer tells us," were his words to Brask, "that he has married a woman to whom he was engaged, and who against her will was made a nun. We see no wrong in such a practice, and wonder much that you did not inform yourself before the girl received her consecration. The husband informs us, further, that you have placed them both beneath the ban. This course appears to us unjust, and we command you to remit the punishment.... We think it better to allow this marriage than to drive the woman to an impure life." A little later, when revolt arose in Dalarne, Gustav fancied that he saw the bishop's hand. "The priests," he said to one of his officers, "are at the bottom of all rebellion, and the diocese of Linköping is the heart of this conspiracy." Gustav had no ground for this suspicion, and the charge was utterly untrue. Brask thought the tax imposed upon the Dalesmen altogether too severe, and did not hesitate to say so; but he was very far from sympathizing with the rebels, and when it was ordered that the diet should be held in Vesterås to please the Dalesmen, he was the first person to suggest a danger in holding it so near the seat of the revolt.

Brask's influential position in the diet only added to the monarch's wrath, and it was against him chiefly that the diet's acts were framed. He was the wealthiest of the Swedish bishops. Hence the reduction in their incomes, as commanded by the diet, fell heaviest on him. But even here the monarch's greed was not assuaged. After the "Ordinantia" had been passed, Gustav rose and called upon the several bishops to resign their castles. This step, though advocated by the burghers and mountaineers as well as common people, had not been ordered by the diet. Gustav seems, therefore, to have made the demand upon his own authority alone, and the issue proved that his authority was great. The bishops of Strengnäs and Skara, on whom the demand was made first, acquiesced as gracefully as was possible to so provoking a demand. But when the monarch came to Brask, that prelate did not readily comply. One of the nobility addressed the king, and begged him to allow the aged bishop to retain his castle during the few short years that yet remained to him of life. This reasonable request, however, the monarch would not grant; and Brask persisting in his right to hold the castle, Gustav deprived him of his retinue and held him prisoner till he furnished bail conditioned for his good behavior as well as for the surrender of his castle. The diet then adjourned, Gustav sending forth a body of men who entered the bishop's castle by main force, and placed it under the supremacy of the king.

The ground of this barbaric treatment appears in a negotiation between the king and Brask some five weeks later. By the Vesterås Recess Gustav was given a claim to all the income not needed by the bishops, cathedrals, and chapters for their support. But since the sum required for the prelates was not named, the field thus left for argument was wide. The prelates took a much higher view of their necessities than was taken by the king. Brask especially found it hard to do without his ancient pomp and circumstance. Gustav therefore put the screws upon him to bring the lordly bishop to the ground. How well this plan succeeded is shown in a document of the 2d of August—about five weeks after the seizure of Brask's castle—in which the bishop is declared to have come to an understanding, and to have promised the king fifteen hundred marks a year beside some other tribute. In reward for this concession, Gustav declared himself contented, and received the bishop once more into royal favor.

There is now but little more to chronicle about the aged bishop. Beaten at every point, and practically a prisoner at the monarch's mercy, he had at last capitulated and granted to Gustav all that he had asked. The surrender, furthermore, was but the prelude to the bishop's flight. Conscious that every hope was crushed forever, he craved permission to visit Gotland and perform the sacred duties of his office. This request was granted, and the venerable prelate set forth never to return. On pretext of consulting eminent physicians, he sailed across the Baltic, and watched the monarch's movements from afar. Gustav, when he learned of this escape, confiscated all the property of Brask that he could find, and, worse than all, he issued a letter, filled with venom, denouncing the perfidy of the aged bishop and telling the people of his diocese that

Brask had fled because of suits that certain persons were about to bring against him for his wrongs.

It is difficult to take our leave of Brask without a word in admiration of his character. He was, in point of intellect, the most commanding figure of his time. Though born and bred among a people strangely void of understanding, he displayed some talents by which he would have stood conspicuous in any court of Europe. His learning possibly was not so great as that of Magni, nor did his eloquence by any means compare with that of Petri. But in matters of diplomacy, in the art of comprehendinghuman nature, he was unsurpassed by any prelate of the day. He was singularly acute in forming his conclusions. Rarely if ever did he express opinions that were not ultimately verified by facts. His versatility, moreover, was something marvellous. While weighted down with every sort of trouble and anxiety, he spent his leisure moments in writing perfectly delightful letters to his friends. These letters bear the marks of suffering, but are calm in spirit, charitable, and replete with thought. They treat of botany, of geographical experiments, and of various schemes to benefit the Swedish nation. As specimens of literature they are superior to any other documents of the time; and the writer evidently took keen pleasure in their composition. "By means of letters," he declared, "we keep our friends; and I would rather keep the friends I have than make new ones." Brask's greatest fault was his hypocrisy; but even this was due more to his education than to any innate trait. He was a Romanist of the deepest dye, and along with Romanism he inherited a tendency to sacrifice the means in order to effect the end. His very earnestness impelled him to deceive. But his deception, if only we may judge him leniently, was of a very pardonable kind. Take him for all in all, he was an extremely interesting man; and when he left the country, Sweden lost a valuable son.

CORONATION OF THE KING. 1528.

THERE is but one scene needed now to bring the drama of the Swedish Revolution to its close. During a period of over four eventful years Gustav Vasa had been seated on the throne, but the final act deemed necessary in the election of a king had not yet taken place. Again and again the people had urged Gustav to be crowned, but on one pretext or another he had put them off, and the ancient rite of coronation was not yet performed. The mystery of this strange delay can easily be explained by looking for a moment into the condition of the Swedish Church.

It was a time-honored theory all over Christendom that no person could be legally installed in any royal post without first having the sanction of the Church of Rome; and such sanction, it was held, could only be conferred through the consecrated archbishop of the land. When Gustav was elected king, the Swedish archbishop was in voluntary exile, and nobody expected that he ever would return. Indeed, he was so far an object of suspicion at the papal court that, shortly after the election of Gustav, the pope appointed another prelate to perform the duties of archbishop till the charges brought against Gustaf Trolle should be set at rest. It is matter of common knowledge that Trolle never succeeded in vindicating his position; and Magni, though not confirmed, continued to perform the duties of archbishop.

In January, 1526, the Cabinet urged Gustav to be crowned, and he declared that he would do so in the coming summer, trusting presumably that Magni would receive his confirmation ere that time. A tax was even levied to defray the expenses of the ceremony. But some opposition was encountered when the royal officers endeavored to collect the tax, and, the kingdom being then in need of revenue, the project had to be postponed. There is evidence, moreover, that Gustav was not eager for the confirmation of the prelates. On one occasion he expressed a fear that they were seeking to obtain their consecration with a view to transfer their allegiance from himself to Rome. Apparently his object was, by continual postponement of the coronation, to have a standing argument whenever he desired to obtain new funds.

Matters therefore dragged on in the same way till Archbishop Magni had been banished and the diet of Vesterås had voted an addition to the income of the king. As the Cabinet had been beyond all others urgent in their solicitations, the announcement of the monarch's resolution was addressed to them. He would have still preferred, he said, to delay his coronation till the summer of 1528; but fearing that at that time he should be too busy, he had resolved to have the rite performed soon after Christmas, and the day he fixed at January 6. Invitations were then sent out to all the noblemen of the realm, who were instructed also to appear with all their retinues, and to bring their wives and daughters with them. Each town was asked to send two delegates to the coronation, and a certain number of persons were to represent the different parishes throughout the land. Sheep, geese, and hens were ordered in enormous quantities to be collected by the royal stewards for the festival. These the thrifty monarch arranged should be provided by the parishes themselves. Lest the Dalesmen, already somewhat irritated, should have new cause for discontent, Gustav wrote them that they need not take part in the contribution, nor even send their representatives if they did not feel inclined.

Although the Swedish Church was practically severed from the Church of Rome, a doubt still lingered in the monarch's mind as to the propriety of a coronation by prelates whose authority had not been sanctioned by the pope. Therefore, to remove all chance of contest, he directed that those bishops who had not received their confirmation should be sanctified through laying on of hands by those who had. As a matter of fact the only bishops whose authority had been derived from Rome were the bishops of Vexiö and Vesterås. The former was too old to undertake the active duties of his office. The bishop of Vesterås was selected, therefore, to consecrate the bishops of Skara, Strengnäs, and Åbo. This was effected on the 5th of January,—just before the coronation festival began.

The gorgeous ceremony was performed, according to ancient

practice, in the Cathedral of Upsala. Representatives from every portion of the realm were present, and the huge edifice was filled from choir to nave with all the wealth and beauty that the land could boast. It was the final tribute of gratitude to one whose ceaseless energy had saved the nation from long years of tyranny. Never had the Swedish people been more deeply bounden to revere their ruler. If in the annals of all history a king deserved to wear a crown, Gustav Vasa was that king. The honor, however, was not all his own. The ceremony of coronation over, Gustav selected from among his courtiers twelve to whom he granted the degree of knighthood. Here again, as on the day of his election, he displayed the sentiments that inspired his whole reign. No longer do we find among the monarch's chosen counsellors the names of men illustrious in the Church and Chapter. It was from the ranks of the lower classes that the persons whom he was to knight were chosen, and from this time forward the knights to all intents and purposes composed his Cabinet. No stronger argument can be offered to show the utter humiliation of the Church.

The act of coronation was followed by a period of mirth. A rich repast was offered by the king, at which the representatives of all the classes were invited to be present. A new coin, also, bearing the full-length figure of Gustav, with his sword and sceptre, and wearing on his head a crown, was issued and distributed gratuitously among the people. On the following days the ceremony was prolonged by tilt and tourney. With all the gallantry of a warmer climate two gladiators entered the lists to combat for the hand of one of Sweden's high-born ladies. The chronicler has immortalized the combatants, but the fair lady's name, by reason of a blemish in the manuscript, is gone forever. From beginning to end the scene was one which no eyewitness ever could forget. Years later, it stirred the spirit of the author whose zeal has given us the leading features of our narrative. It is a fitting picture with which to close this tale.

The Swedish Revolution now was at an end, and the great achievements of Gustav Vasa had been done. Though not yet thirty-two, the youthful monarch had already secured a place among the foremost leaders of the world. We have watched the Swedish nation rise from insignificance, through a series of remarkable developments, till its grandeur cast a lengthened shadow across the face of northern Europe. In some regards this revolution stands pre-eminent above all others known in history. Few political upheavals have been more sudden, and few, if any, have been more complete. Seven years was all Gustav needed to annihilate the ancient constitution, and fashion another structure of an absolutely new design. The Cabinet, at one time the autocrat of Sweden, was now a mere puppet in the monarch's hand. Under the guise of leader of the people, Gustav had crushed the magnates, with all their old magnificence and power, beneath his feet. In place of bishops and archbishops, whose insolence had been to former kings a constant menace, his court was filled with common soldiers selected from the body of the nation, and raised to posts of highest honor, for no other reason than their obedience to the monarch's will. Of the old ecclesiastical authority not a trace was left. Rome, in ages past the ultimate tribunal for the nation, had now no more to say in Sweden than in the kingdom of Japan. The Reformation was so thorough that from the reign of Gustav Vasa to the present day, it is asserted, no citizen of Sweden has become a Romish priest.

The Revolution whose main incidents have here been followed recalls another Revolution enacted near three centuries later amid the forests of the great continent of North America. Both originated in a long series of acts of tyranny, and each gave birth to a hero whose name has become a lasting synonym of strength and greatness. The lessons of history, however, are more often found in contrasts than in similarities, and the points of difference between these two upheavals are no less striking than their points of likeness. The chief difference lies in the individual characteristics of the leaders. George Washington was pre-eminently a hero of the people. He embraced the popular cause from no other motive than a love of what he deemed the people's rights; and when the war of independence closed, he retired from public life and allowed the nation whose battle he had fought to take the government of the country upon itself. The result was the most perfect system of republican government that the world has ever known. Gustav Vasa, on the other hand, though actuated in a measure by enthusiasm for the public weal, was driven into the contest mainly by a necessity to save himself. The calm disinterestedness which marks the career of Washington was wholly wanting in the Swedish king. His readiness to debase the currency, his efforts to humiliate the bishops, his confiscation of Church property, his intimacy with foreign courtiers,—all show a desire for personal aggrandizement inconsistent with an earnest longing to benefit his race. One must regret that the rare talents which he possessed, and the brilliant opportunities that lay before him, were not employed in more unselfish ends. It is true he gave his country a better constitution than it had before; he freed it from the atrocities of a horrid tyrant; he laid the axe at the root of many religious absurdities; and he relieved the people from a heavy load of religious burdens. But he did not lay that foundation of public liberty which the blood poured out by the Swedish people merited. Of all nations on the face of the globe none are more fitted by temperament for a republican form of government than the Swedes. They are calm, they are thoughtful, they are economical, and above all else, they are imbued with an ardent love of liberty. It is hard, therefore, to repress the wish that Gustav Vasa had been allowed, at the diet of Vesterås, to lay aside the crown, and that in his place a leader had been chosen to carry on the good work on the lines already drawn. The Revolution had begun with a feeling that the Swedish nation was entitled to be ruled according to its ancient laws,—that it was entitled to a representative form of government; and it was only because of the nation's admiration for its leader that this object was relinquished. The people, having expelled one tyrant, chose another; and ere Gustav closed his memorable reign, the principle of hereditary monarchy was once more engrafted on the nation. Nothing could demonstrate with greater clearness the extreme danger that is always imminent in blind enthusiasm for a popular and gifted leader.

Made in United States
North Haven, CT
29 January 2024

48059600R00095